Pocket
BANGKOK
TOP SIGHTS • LOCAL LIFE • MADE EASY

Austin Bush

In This Book

QuickStart Guide

Your keys to understanding the city – we help you decide what to do and how to do it

Need to Know
Tips for a smooth trip

Neighbourhoods
What's where

Explore Bangkok

The best things to see and do, neighbourhood by neighbourhood

Top Sights
Make the most of your visit

Local Life
The insider's city

The Best of Bangkok

The city's highlights in handy lists to help you plan

Best Walks
See the city on foot

Bangkok's Best...
The best experiences

Survival Guide

Tips and tricks for a seamless, hassle-free city experience

Getting Around
Travel like a local

Essential Information
Including where to stay

Our selection of the city's best places to eat, drink and experience:

◎ **Sights**

✖ **Eating**

🖥 **Drinking**

✪ Entertainment

🔒 **Shopping**

These symbols give you the vital information for each listing:

- ☏ Telephone Numbers
- ⊙ Opening Hours
- P Parking
- ⊖ Nonsmoking
- 🌐 Internet Access
- 🛜 Wi-Fi Access
- 🌱 Vegetarian Selection
- 📖 English-Language Menu
- 👪 Family-Friendly
- 🐾 Pet-Friendly
- 🚌 Bus
- 🛳 Ferry
- Ⓜ Metro
- Ⓢ Skytrain (BTS)
- 🚊 Tram
- 🚆 Train

Find each listing quickly on maps for each neighbourhood:

Bar Hemingway

16 🖥 Map p233, B2

Legend has it that Hem... self, wielding a machine ...rate this timber-pan... ...ered bar during ... showpiece is a ...en by Papa a... town. Dress ...s.com; Hôtel Rit... ⊙ 6.30pm-2a...

6 ◎ Plac...

Lonely Planet's Bangkok

Lonely Planet Pocket Guides are designed to get you straight to the heart of the city.

Inside you'll find all the must-see sights, plus tips to make your visit to each one really memorable. We've split the city into easy-to-navigate neighbourhoods and provided clear maps so you'll find your way around with ease. Our expert authors have searched out the best of the city: walks, food, nightlife and shopping, to name a few. Because you want to explore, our 'Local Life' pages will take you to some of the most exciting areas to experience the real Bangkok.

And of course you'll find all the practical tips you need for a smooth trip: itineraries for short visits, how to get around, and how much to tip the guy who serves you a drink at the end of a long day's exploration.

It's your guarantee of a really great experience.

Our Promise

You can trust our travel information because Lonely Planet authors visit the places we write about, each and every edition. We never accept freebies for positive coverage, so you can rely on us to tell it like it is.

QuickStart Guide 7

Explore Bangkok 21

Worth a Trip:

The Best of Bangkok **145**

Bangkok's Best Walks

Bangkok's Best ...

Survival Guide **171**

QuickStart Guide

Welcome to Bangkok

Scratch Bangkok's surface and you'll find a city with mega-malls minutes from 200-year-old homes, temples sharing space with neon-lit strips of sleaze, and food cart–lined streets overlooked by bars perched on skyscrapers. As Bangkok races towards the future, these quirks will continue to supply the city with its unique brand of Thai-ness.

Street shrine, Bangkok
RICHARD I'ANSON / GETTY IMAGES ©

Bangkok
Top Sights

Wat Phra Kaew & Grand Palace (p24)

Easily the most ostentatious temple in Thailand, Wat Phra Kaew blows minds with its blinged-out structures and Emerald Buddha. Next door, the Grand Palace is the equally decadent former residence of Thailand's royal family.

JEAN-PIERRE LESCOURRET / GETTY IMAGES ©

Wat Pho (p28)

At nearly 50m long and 15m high, it's impossible not to be awed by Wat Pho's reclining Buddha. If you require more than just girth, the grounds are also home to a traditional massage school.

Jim Thompson House (p78)

The eponymous American silk entrepreneur mysteriously disappeared in 1967. His Thai-style former home lives on as a visit-worthy repository for ageing local traditions and artwork.

Chatuchak Weekend Market (p136)

In a city obsessed with commerce, Chatuchak takes the prize as Bangkok's biggest and baddest market. Silks, sneakers, fighting fish and fluffy puppies – if it can be sold in Thailand, you'll find it here.

INGOLF POMPE / GETTY IMAGES ©

Wat Arun (p32)

It's the setting by the river, rather than the gold or Buddha statues, that draws most folks here. And justifiably: the views are great and Wat Arun is one of the few temples visitors can climb on.

ANUCHIT KAM-SONGMUEANG / GETTY IMAGES ©

Ko Kret (p142)

Leave the city behind at this artificial yet thoroughly rural-feeling island in Mae Nam Chao Phraya. Arrive on a weekend and combine your excursion with a busy open-air market and unique eats.

JOHN BORTHWICK / GETTY IMAGES ©

Wat Traimit (Golden Buddha) (p62)

All the gold in Chinatown (and believe us, there's a lot) would scarcely be enough to recreate this nearly 6-ton, solid-gold Buddha image. Let the jaw-dropping begin at this temple in Bangkok's Chinatown.

Dusit Palace Park (p58)

Witness Victorian sense and Thai sensibilities merging in this former royal enclave. Visit museums and the world's largest teak building, or simply take advantage of Dusit Palace Park's green setting – itself an anomaly in Bangkok

Ayuthaya (p140)

The remains of the once decadent capital of Siam are now a Unesco World Heritage Site, and an easy (and must-do) day trip from Bangkok.

Bangkok
Local Life

Insider tips to help you find the real city

Don't want to feel like a sheltered package holidaymaker? Rest assured that it's a cinch to get local in Bangkok, a city where hectic tourist attractions often rub shoulders with classic local neighbourhoods.

Banglamphu Pub Crawl (p42)

▶ Fun bars
▶ Live music

Bangkok's most traditional 'hood is also one of its best for nightlife. Parts of Banglamphu can feel dominated by the backpacker magnet that is Th Khao San, but just off the main strip are heaps of bars and restaurants frequented mostly by young locals.

A Taste of Chinatown (p64)

▶ Street food
▶ Urban exploration

Many places in Chinatown have neither roof nor menu, but it's not unusual for locals to brave traffic, heat or rain for a meal here. Not surprisingly, Chinese-style dishes rule – think noodles, pork and fried dishes – but seafood, sweets and fruit also have their places.

Gay Silom (p98)

▶ Gay bars
▶ Gay dance clubs

Come night-time, gay visitors and locals alike flock to the side streets off lower Th Silom. The alternatives run the gamut from seedy go-go bars to sophisticated dance clubs – and just about everything in between.

Victory Monument & Around (p94)

▶ Live music
▶ Regional Thai food

Want a taste of provincial Thailand without leaving Bangkok? Head to this suburban 'hood known for its main landmark. Here you'll find fun bars, live music and good food, from bars boasting wine and cheese to street-side stalls hawking northeastern Thai specialities – all served up without a hint of big-city pretension.

RCA (Royal City Avenue) (p116)

▶ Dance clubs
▶ Live music

Hands-down the city's premier nightlife strip; RCA's clubs were formerly a teen scene, but the area has grown up in recent years. Today it draws a wide spectrum of partiers, not to mention a hearty selection of music, from live pop to big-name DJs.

JOHN BORTHWICK / GETTY IMAGES ©

Above: Chao Phraya cruise; **Below:** Opera performer, Vegetarian Festival

IGOR BILIC / GETTY IMAGES ©

Other great places to experience the city like a local:

MBK Food Island (p86)

Amulet Market (p39)

Asia Herb Association (p129)

Thanon Bamrung Meuang (p57)

Chao Phraya Dinner Cruise (p108)

Paragon Cineplex (p90)

Vegetarian Festival (p73)

ThaiCraft Fair (p133)

Raja's Fashions (p134)

Bangkok
Day Planner

Day One

Get up as early as you can to take the Chao Phraya Express Boat to Tha Chang to explore Ko Ratanakosin's must-see temples: **Wat Phra Kaew & Grand Palace** (p24), **Wat Pho** (p28) and **Wat Arun** (p32). For lunch, take the plunge into authentic Bangkok-style cuisine at **Ming Lee** (p146) or **Pa Aew** (p37).

Refresh with a spa treatment at **Health Land** (p103), or soothe overworked legs with a traditional Thai massage at **Ruen-Nuad Massage Studio** (p102). After freshening up, get a new perspective on Bangkok with rooftop cocktails at **Moon Bar** (p109).

For dinner, **nahm** (p105) serves what is arguably some of the best Thai food in Bangkok. If you've still got it in you, get dancing at **Tapas Room** (p110), or head over to **Telephone Pub** (p98) or any of the other bars in Bangkok's lively gaybourhood. For a night that doesn't end until the sun comes up, bang on the door at **Smalls** (p109).

Day Two

Take the BTS (Skytrain) to National Stadium and start your day with a visit to the popular and worthwhile museum **Jim Thompson House** (p78). Afterwards, check out the latest exhibition at the **Bangkok Art & Culture Centre** (p82).

Lunch at the nearby **MBK Food Island** (p86), a thorough and cheap introduction to Thai food. After eating, walk, or let the BTS escort you, through Bangkok's ultramodern commercial district, stopping off at linked shopping centres **MBK Center** (p91), **Siam Center** (p91) and **Siam Square** (p92). Be sure to throw in a prayer for good luck at the **Erawan Shrine** (p82).

Come dinnertime, give your credit card a break and become acquainted with rustic Thai food at **Kai Thort Jay Kee** (p106). If it's a Friday or Saturday night, make a point of schlepping over to RCA (Royal City Avenue) and the fun clubs there such as **Route 66** (p117) or **Slim** (p117). If it's a weekday, consider the stage show at **Playhouse Theater Cabaret** (p91) or live music at **Titanium** (p132).

Short on time?
We've arranged Bangkok's must-sees into these day-by-day itineraries to make sure you see the very best of the city in the time you have available.

Day Three

☀ Take the *klorng* (canal; also spelt *khlong*) boat to Banglamphu, where you'll spend the first half of your day peeking into low-key but visit-worthy temples such as the **Golden Mount & Wat Saket** (p46) and **Wat Suthat** (p46). Swing through the artisan village **Ban Baat** (p46), then visit the bizarre strip of religious commerce that is **Thanon Bamrung Meuang** (p57).

☀ Have lunch at the equally homey and lauded Thai restaurant **Krua Apsorn** (p49). Spend the afternoon in the famous backpacker melting pot of Th Khao San, people-watching and picking up souvenirs at **Thanon Khao San Market** (p57).

☾ For dinner, head over to Th Sukhumvit and take a temporary break from Thai food at one of this strip's great international restaurants, such as **Jidori-Ya Kenzou** (p122) or **Nasir Al-Masri** (p125). End the night with a Thai-themed cocktail at a cosy local such as **WTF** (p128) or **Tuba** (p128), or a street-side Singha at **Cheap Charlie's** (p130). If it's still too early to head in, extend the night with dancing at **Grease** (p130) or live music at **Apoteka** (p133).

Day Four

☀ If it's a weekend, take the BTS north for a half-day of shopping at the **Chatuchak Weekend Market** (p136). Otherwise, take a half-day excursion outside the city to the artificial island of **Ko Kret** (p142), or a day trip to **Ayuthaya** (p140).

☀ Take time to recover from the market (or your excursion), and in the relative cool of the late afternoon take the MRT (metro) to Chinatown and visit the home of the Golden Buddha, **Wat Traimit** (p62), and the Chinese-style **Wat Mangkon Kamalawat** (p68). Consider popping over to **Phahurat** (p68) to sample that neighbourhood's South Asian feel. Try our food-based **walking tour** (p64) of Chinatown's famous street stalls for dinner.

☾ After dinner, consider heading to **Pak Khlong Talat** (p67), Bangkok's nocturnal flower market. Alternatively, cross to Banglamphu and kick the night off with drinks at **Hippie de Bar** (p53), followed by a rowdy live-music show at **Brick Bar** (p54). If bedtime is irrelevant, head upstairs to the *shishas* (water pipes) and dance floor of **Bank** (p43).

Need to Know

**For more information,
see Survival Guide (p172)**

Currency
Thai baht (B)

Language
Thai

Visas
Most international air arrivals are eligible
for a 30-day visa exemption; 60-day visas
are available from a Thai consulate before
leaving home.

Money
ATMs are widespread and charge a 150B
to 180B foreign-account fee. Visa and
MasterCard are accepted at
upmarket places.

Mobile Phones
Thailand is on a GSM and 3G network
through inexpensive prepaid SIM cards.

Time
Asia/Bangkok (GMT/UTC plus seven hours)

Plugs & Adaptors
Plugs have two-prong round or flat sockets;
electrical current is 220V.

Tipping
Tipping is generally not expected in Thailand.

❶ Before You Go

Your Daily Budget

Budget less than 1500B

▶ Dorm bed or basic guesthouse room
250–600B

▶ Street-stall meals

▶ A couple of the big-hitter sights, supplemented with free temples and parks

Midrange 1500–3000B

▶ Flashpacker guesthouse or midrange hotel
room 800–1500B

▶ Shophouse restaurant meals

▶ Most, if not all, of the big sights

Top End more than 3000B

▶ Boutique hotel room from 2000B

▶ Fine dining

▶ Private tours

Useful Websites

Lonely Planet (www.lonelyplanet.com/
bangkok) Info, hotel bookings and more.

BK (bk.asia-city.com) Online version of
Bangkok's best listings magazine.

Bangkok 101 (www.bangkok101.com)
Tourist-friendly listings mag.

Advance Planning

Three months before Book at a boutique
hotel, especially for December or January.

One month before Apply for a visa at the
Thai embassy or consulate in your home
country if you plan to stay longer than
30 days; make reservations at nahm (p105).

A week before Buy clothes appropriate
for hot weather; book lessons at a Thai
cooking school.

② Arriving in Bangkok

Suvarnabhumi is Bangkok's primary international air hub and is located 25km east of the city centre. Don Muang, Bangkok's low-cost terminal, is north of the city.

✈ From Suvarnabhumi International Airport (BKK)

Destination	Best Transport
Banglamphu, Ko Ratanakosin & Thonburi	taxi, bus 556
Chinatown	taxi, Airport Link (transfer to MRT)
Siam Square	taxi, Airport Link (transfer to BTS)
Riverside, Silom & Lumphini	taxi, Airport Link (transfer to MRT or BTS)

✈ From Don Muang International Airport (DMK)

Destination	Best Transport
Banglamphu, Ko Ratanakosin & Thonburi	taxi, bus 59
Chinatown	taxi, bus 29, train
Siam Square	taxi, bus A1, A2 or 538 (transfer to BTS)
Riverside, Silom & Lumphini	taxi, bus A1 or A2 (transfer to BTS)

③ Getting Around

Bangkok's public transport network is continually growing, but it is still relatively young, and getting to certain parts of the city – particularly the older areas – remains extremely time-consuming. The best strategy is usually to combine a longer trip on the BTS or MRT with a short taxi ride.

S BTS

The elevated Skytrain (www.bts.co.th) is probably the most efficient and convenient way to get around central Bangkok.

M MRT

Bangkok's metro (www.bangkokmetro.co.th) is convenient, although not quite as expansive as the Skytrain network.

🚗 Taxi

Outside peak hours, Bangkok taxis are a great bargain.

⛵ Chao Phraya Express Boat

These boats (www.chaophrayaexpressboat.com.th) are a slow but steady way to visit the tourist sights along Mae Nam Chao Phraya.

⛵ Klorng Boat

Bangkok's canal boats are generally more useful for commuters than visitors.

🚌 Bus

Bangkok's buses (www.bmta.co.th) are a cheap but slow and confusing way to get around the city.

Bangkok
Neighbourhoods

Banglamphu (p40)
Despite being home to the intergalactic melting pot that is Th Khao San, this district of antique shophouses and temples remains the city's most characteristically 'Bangkok' neighbourhood.

Ko Ratanakosin & Thonburi (p22)
Bangkok's riverside historical centre includes the monuments to king, country and religion that draw most tourists.

Top Sights
Wat Phra Kaew & Grand Palace

Wat Pho

Wat Arun

Dusit Palace Park

Wat Phra Kaew & Grand Palace

Jim Thompson House

Wat Pho

Wat Arun

Wat Traimit (Golden Buddha)

Chinatown (p60)
Home to shark-fin restaurants, gaudy gold and jade shops, and flashing neon signs in Chinese characters, Chinatown is Bangkok's most hectic neighbourhood.

Top Sights
Wat Traimit (Golden Buddha)

Chatuchak Weekend Market

Siam Square, Pratunam & Ploenchit (p76)

The area around Siam Square is essentially one giant shopping mall, and today is considered the unofficial centre of modern Bangkok.

Top Sights

Jim Thompson House

Worth a Trip

Top Sights

Chatuchak Weekend Market

Dusit Palace Park

Ko Kret

Ayuthaya

Sukhumvit (p118)

Dominating the area east of central Bangkok is Sukhumvit, a busy commercial and residential neighbourhood with modern midrange hotels. It's a favourite of expatriates and cosmopolitan Thais.

Riverside, Silom & Lumphini (p96)

This is Bangkok's de facto financial district, and most locals come here to work, while you'll probably come to eat, play or stay.

Explore
Bangkok

Wat Phra Kaew and Grand Palace (p24)
JAN WLODARCZYK / GETTY IMAGES ©

Explore

Ko Ratanakosin & Thonburi

The artificial island of Ko Ratanakosin is Bangkok's birthplace, and the Buddhist temples and royal palaces here comprise some of the city's most important and most visited sights. By contrast, Thonburi, located across Mae Nam Chao Phraya (Chao Phraya River), is a seemingly forgotten yet visit-worthy zone of sleepy residential districts connected by *klorng* (canals; also spelt *khlong*).

C HUANG / GETTY IMAGES ©

The Sights in a Day

Get an early start – to take advantage of the cooler weather and to beat the crowds – and begin your day at what is arguably Bangkok's premier sight, **Wat Phra Kaew & Grand Palace** (p24). Then make the short walk next door and feel your jaw drop to the floor at the sight of the immense reclining Buddha at **Wat Pho** (p28).

You'll probably be tired, hungry and hot at this point, so recharge at the graciously air-conditioned **Coconut Palm** (p37). After lunch, stop in for a massage at **Chetawan Traditional Massage School** (p36) or, if intellectual rather than physical stimulation is your thing, investigate the fun exhibits at the **Museum of Siam** (p35) or the ancient treasures at the **National Museum** (p35).

Come late afternoon, cross Mae Nam Chao Phraya and climb around on **Wat Arun** (p32). Coordinate your return to Ko Ratanakosin with sunset cocktails at **Roof** (p38) before dinner at a riverside restaurant such as **Sala Rattanakosin** (p38) or **Khunkung** (p37).

 Top Sights

Wat Phra Kaew & Grand Palace (p24)

Wat Pho (p28)

Wat Arun (p32)

Best of Bangkok

Temples

Wat Phra Kaew (p24)

Wat Pho (p28)

Wat Arun (p32)

Museums

Museum of Siam (p35)

National Museum (p35)

Songkran Niyomsane Forensic Medicine Museum & Parasite Museum (p36)

Rooftop Bars

Roof (p38)

Amorosa (p39)

Getting There

River ferry To Ko Ratanakosin: Tha Tien and Tha Chang. To Thonburi: Tha Wang Lang/Siriraj and Tha Saphan Phra Pin Klao.

S BTS To Thonburi: Krung Thonburi or Wong Wian Yai and taxi.

Top Sights
Wat Phra Kaew & Grand Palace

Also known as the Temple of the Emerald Buddha, Wat Phra Kaew is the colloquial name of the vast fairy-tale compound that also includes the former residence of the Thai monarch, the Grand Palace. The ground was consecrated in 1782, the first year of Bangkok rule, and is today Bangkok's biggest tourist attraction and a pilgrimage destination for devout Buddhists and nationalists. The 94.5-hectare grounds encompass more than 100 buildings that represent 200 years of royal history and architectural experimentation.

วัดพระแก้ว,
พระบรมมหาราชวัง

◉ Map p34, C4

Th Na Phra Lan

admission 500B

⊙ 8.30am-3.30pm

⛴ Tha Chang

Don't Miss

The Emerald Buddha

On a tall platform in Wat Phra Kaew's fantastically decorated *bòht* (ordination hall), the Emerald Buddha is the temple's primary attraction. Despite the name, the statue is actually carved from a single piece of nephrite, a type of jade. The diminutive figure (it's only 66cm tall) is always cloaked in royal robes, one for each season (hot, cool and rainy).

Some time in the 15th century, the Emerald Buddha is said to have been covered with plaster and gold leaf, and placed in Chiang Rai's own Wat Phra Kaew. Many valuable Buddha images were masked in this way to deter potential thieves and marauders during unstable times. Often the true identity of the image was forgotten over the years until a 'divine accident' exposed its precious core. The Emerald Buddha experienced such a divine revelation while it was being transported to a new location. In a fall, the plaster covering broke off, revealing the brilliant green inside.

Later, during territorial clashes with Laos during the mid-16th century, the Emerald Buddha was seized and taken to modern-day Laos. Some 200 years later, the Thai army marched up to Vientiane, razed the city and hauled off the Emerald Buddha. The Buddha was enshrined in the then capital, Thonburi, before the general who led the sacking of Vientiane assumed the throne and had it moved to its present location.

The *bòht* itself is a notable example of the Ratanakosin school of architecture, which combines stylistic holdovers from Ayuthaya along with modern touche s from China and the West.

JOHN W BANAGAN / GETTY IMAGES ©

☑ Top Tips

▶ Enter Wat Phra Kaew and the Grand Palace complex through the clearly marked third gate from the river pier. Tickets are purchased inside the complex; anyone telling you it's closed is a gem tout or con artist.

▶ At Wat Phra Kaew and the Grand Palace grounds, dress rules are strictly enforced. If you're flashing a bit too much skin, expect to be shown into a dressing room and issued with a shirt or sarong (rental is free, but you must provide a refundable 200B deposit).

▶ Admission to the complex includes entrance to Dusit Palace Park (p59).

✗ Take a Break

Cap off your visit to Wat Phra Kaew and the Grand Palace with lunch at Ming Lee (p37), a charmingly old-school Thai restaurant located virtually across the street from the complex's main entrance.

Ramakian Murals

Recently restored murals of the *Ramakian* (the Thai version of the Indian epic the *Ramayana*) line the inside walls of the Wat Phra Kaew compound. Originally painted during the reign of Rama I (King Phraphut-thayotfa; r 1782–1809), the 178 sections, beginning at the north gate and moving clockwise around the compound, describe the struggles of Rama to rescue his kidnapped wife, Sita.

Guardians of Wat Phra Kaew

The first sights you'll see upon entering Wat Phra Kaew are two 5m-high *yaksha*, giants or ogres with origins in Hindu/Buddhist mythology. Other mythical creatures in the temple compound include the half-human, half-bird *kinnaree* and the sacred birds known as *garuda*, not to mention various hermits and elephants.

Phra Mondop

Commissioned by Rama I, this structure was built for the storage of sacred Buddhist manuscripts. The seven-tiered roof, floor woven from strands of silver, and intricate mother-of-pearl door panels make it among the world's most decadent libraries. The interior of Phra Mondop is closed to the public.

Phra Mondop, along with the neighbouring Khmer-style peak of the Prasat Phra Thep Bidon and the gilded Phra Si Ratana *chedi* (stupa), are the tallest structures in the compound.

Chakri Mahaprasat

The largest of the Grand Palace buildings is the Chakri Mahaprasat (Grand Palace Hall). Completed in 1882 following a plan by British architects, the exterior shows a blend of Italian Renaissance and traditional Thai architecture that earned it the nickname *fa·ràng sài chá·dah* (Westerner in a Thai crown). The central spire contains the ashes of Chakri kings; the flanking spires enshrine the ashes of the Chakri princes who failed to inherit the throne.

Amarindra Hall

Originally a hall of justice, this large, mostly empty hall is used for coronation ceremonies – the most recent occasion being the current king's coronation in 1950. The golden, boat-shaped throne looks considerably more ornate than comfortable.

Borombhiman Hall

This French-inspired structure served as a residence for Rama VI (King Vajiravudh; r 1910–25). The palace was where Rama VIII (King Ananda Mahidol; r 1935–46) was mysteriously killed in 1946, and in April 1981 General San Chitpatima used it as the headquarters for an attempted coup. Today the structure can only be viewed through its iron gates.

Dusit Hall

The compound's westernmost structure is the Ratanakosin-style Dusit Hall, which initially served as a venue for royal audiences and later as a royal funerary hall.

Wat Phra Kaew & Grand Palace

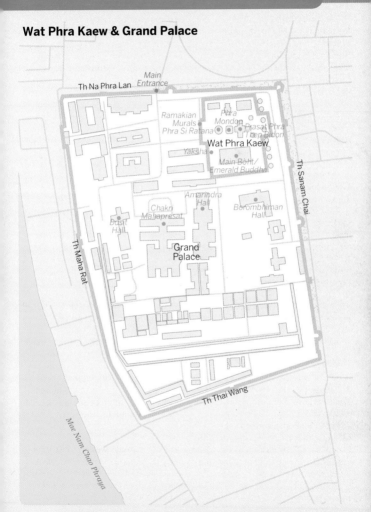

Top Sights
Wat Pho

Of all Bangkok's temples, Wat Pho is arguably the one most worth visiting, for its remarkable reclining Buddha image alone. Yet its sprawling, stupa-studded grounds boast a long list of superlatives: the oldest and largest wát in Bangkok, the longest reclining Buddha, the largest collection of Buddha images in Thailand, and the country's first public education institution. For all that, it sees (slightly) fewer visitors than neighbouring Wat Phra Kaew and feels less commercial.

วัดโพธิ์/วัดพระเชตุพน
Wat Phra Chetuphon

◉ Map p34, D5

Th Sanam Chai

admission 200B

⊙ 8.30am-6.30pm

🛥 Tha Tien

Reclining Buddha

Don't Miss

Reclining Buddha

Located in the compound's main *wí·hǎhn* (sanctuary), the genuinely impressive Reclining Buddha, 46m long and 15m high, illustrates the passing of the Buddha into nirvana (ie the Buddha's death). Completed in 1848 and still holding the title of Bangkok's largest Reclining Buddha, the figure is modelled out of plaster around a brick core and is finished in gold leaf. Mother-of-pearl inlay ornaments the feet, displaying the 108 different auspicious *lák·sà·nà* (characteristics) of a Buddha. Continuing the numerical theme, behind the statue are 108 bronze monk bowls; for 20B you can buy 108 coins, each of which is dropped in a bowl for good luck.

Massage

At what other sacred religious sight in the world can you get a massage? Wat Pho is the national headquarters for the teaching of traditional Thai medicine, which includes Thai massage. The famous massage school has two **massage pavilions** (Thai massage per hour 420B; ⏱8am-6pm) located within the temple compound and additional rooms within a training facility (p36) outside the temple.

Phra Ubosot

Though built during the reign of Rama I and influenced by the Ayuthaya school of architecture, the *bòht* (ordination hall) as it stands today is the result of extensive renovations dating back to the reign of Rama III (King Phranangklao; r 1824–51). Inside you'll find impressive murals and a three-tiered pedestal supporting Phra Buddha Deva Patimakorn, the compound's second-most noteworthy Buddha statue, as well as the ashes of Rama I.

JON BOWER AT APEXPHOTOS / GETTY IMAGES ©

☑ **Top Tips**

▶ Arrive early to avoid the crowds and to take advantage of the (relatively) cool weather.

▶ Don't just gawk at the Reclining Buddha and call it a day: Wat Pho's fantastical, almost mazelike grounds are also part of the experience, and are home to some less hyped but worthwhile treasures.

▶ If you're hot and footsore, the air-conditioned massage pavilions near Wat Pho's east gate could be a welcome way to cool down while experiencing high-quality and relatively inexpensive Thai massage.

✖ **Take a Break**

Convenient and delicious refreshment after your temple visit (or massage) can be obtained at the upscale Sala Rattanakosin (p38) or the more casual Coconut Palm (p37).

Other Buddha Statues

The images on display in the four *wí·hǎhn* surrounding Phra Ubosot are worth investigation. Particularly beautiful are the Phra Chinnarat and Phra Chinnasri Buddhas in the western and southern *wí·hǎhn*, both recovered from Sukhothai by relatives of Rama I. The galleries extending between the four structures feature no fewer than 394 gilded Buddha images spanning nearly all schools of traditional Thai craftsmanship, from Lopburi to Ko Ratanakosin.

Ancient Inscriptions

Encircling Phra Ubosot is a low marble wall with 152 bas-reliefs depicting scenes from the *Ramakian*. You'll recognise some of these figures when you exit the temple past the hawkers with mass-produced rubbings for sale; these are made from cement casts based on Wat Pho's reliefs.

Nearby, a small pavilion has Unesco-recognised inscriptions detailing the tenets of traditional Thai massage. These and as many as 2000 other stone inscriptions covering various aspects of traditional Thai knowledge led to Wat Pho's legacy as the country's first public university.

Royal Chedi

On the western side of the grounds a collection of four towering *chedi* (pagodas or stupas) commemorates the first four Chakri kings. Note the square bell shape with distinct corners, a signature of Ratanakosin style, and the tiles emulating the colours of the Buddhist flag. The middle *chedi* is dedicated to Rama I and encases Phra Si Sanphet Dayarn, a 16m-high standing Buddha image recovered from Ayuthaya. The temple compound's 91 smaller *chedi* include clusters containing the ashes of lesser royal descendants.

Understand
Wat Pho's Rock Giants

Aside from monks and sightseers, Wat Pho is filled with an altogether stiffer crowd: dozens of giants and figurines carved from granite. The rock giants first arrived in Thailand as ballast aboard Chinese junks and were put to work in Wat Pho – and other *wát*, including Wat Suthat (p46) – guarding the entrances of temple gates and courtyards. Look closely and you'll see an array of Chinese characters. The giants with bulging eyes and Chinese opera costumes were inspired by warrior noblemen and are called Lan Than. The figure in a straw hat is a farmer, forever interrupted during his day's work cultivating the fields. And can you recognise the guy in the fedora-like hat with a trimmed beard and moustache? Marco Polo, of course, who introduced such European styles to the Chinese court.

Wat Pho

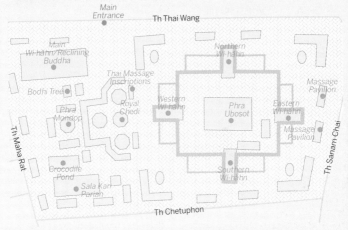

Phra Mondop

Also known as *hŏr đrai*, and serving as a depository for Buddhist scriptures, the elevated Phra Mondop is guarded by four *yaksha* (giants). Legend has it that an argument between the four led to the clearing of the area known today as Tha Tien. Just south of Phra Mondop is the currently reptile-free Crocodile Pond.

Sala Kan Parian

Located in the southwestern corner of the compound is Sala Kan Parian, one of the few remaining structures that predates Rama III's extensive 19th century renovation/expansion of then Wat Pho Tharam. Built in the Ayuthaya style, the structure formerly functioned as the wát's primary *bòht*, and held the temple compound's primary Buddha statue.

The Grounds

Small Chinese-style rock gardens and hill islands interrupt the tiled courtyards, providing shade, greenery and quirky decorations depicting daily life. Keep an eye out for the distinctive rockery festooned with pewter figures of the hermit Khao Mor, who is credited with inventing yoga, in various healing positions. Directly south of the main *wí·hăhn* is a Bodhi tree (*dôn po*), grown from a clipping of the original under which the Buddha is said to have attained enlightenment, and also the source of the temple's colloquial name, Wat Pho.

Top Sights
Wat Arun

The missile-shaped temple that rises from the banks of Mae Nam Chao Phraya is known as the Temple of Dawn, and was named after the Indian god of dawn, Aruna. It was here that King Taksin stumbled upon a shrine and interpreted the discovery as an auspicious sign that this should be the site of the new capital of Siam. Today, Wat Arun is known for its emblematic spire, and is one of the few Buddhist temples visitors can climb on.

วัดอรุณฯ

◉ Map p34, B5

www.watarun.net

off Th Arun Amarin

admission 50B

🕔 8am-6pm

🚢 cross-river ferry from Tha Tien

Don't Miss

The Spire
The central feature of Wat Arun is the 82m-high Khmer-style *brahng* (spire), constructed during the first half of the 19th century. From the river it is not apparent that this steeple is adorned with colourful floral murals made of glazed porcelain, a common temple ornamentation in the early Ratanakosin period, when Chinese ships calling at Bangkok used the stuff as ballast.

The Ordination Hall
The compound's primary *bòht* (ordination hall) contains a Buddha image that is said to have been designed by Rama II (King Phraphutthaloetla Naphalai; r 1809–24) himself, as well as beautiful murals that depict Prince Siddhartha (the Buddha) encountering examples of birth, old age, sickness and death outside his palace walls, experiences that led him to abandon the worldly life.

The Grounds
In addition to the central spire and ordination hall, the Wat Arun compound includes two *wí·hǎhn* (sanctuaries) and a *hǒr drai* (depository for Buddhist scriptures), among other structures. Adjacent to the river are six Chinese-style *sǎh·lah* (often spelt as *sala*), open-air pavilions traditionally meant for relaxing or study, but increasingly used these days as docks for tourist boats.

Exploring the Neighbourhood
Many people visit Wat Arun on long-tail boat tours, but it's dead easy and more rewarding to just jump on the 3B cross-river ferry from Tha Tien (from 5am to 9pm). Once across, consider taking a stroll away from the river on Th Wang Doem, a quiet tiled street of wooden shophouses.

☑ Top Tips

▸ You must wear appropriate clothing to climb on Wat Arun. If you are flashing too much flesh, you'll have to rent a sarong for 20B (and a 100B refundable deposit).

▸ For our money, it's best to visit Wat Arun in the late afternoon, when the sun shines from the west, lighting up the spire and the river behind it.

▸ Sunset views of the temple compound can be caught from across the river at the riverfront warehouses that line Th Maha Rat – although be forewarned that locals may ask for a 20B 'fee'.

✕ Take a Break

If you're visiting Wat Arun at sunset, a great place to soak up the views is Roof (p38), the rooftop bar at the Sala Rattanakosin.

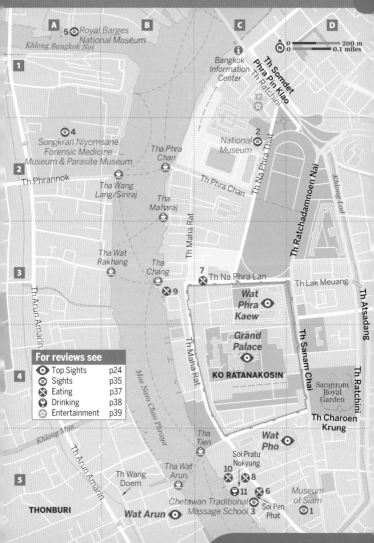

A **B** **C** **D**

5 Royal Barges National Museum

Khlong Bangkok Noi

0 200 m
0 0.1 miles

Th Somdet
Phra Pin Klao

Bangkok Information Center

Th Ratchini

1

12

4
Songkran Niyomsane Forensic Medicine Museum & Parasite Museum

Tha Phra Chan

National Museum

2

Th Phrannok

Tha Wang Lang/Siriraj

Th Na Phra That

Khlong Lot

2

Tha Maharaj

Th Phra Chan

Th Ratchadamnoen Nai

Tha Wat Rakhang

Tha Chang

Th Maha Rat

7 Th Na Phra Lan

Th Lak Meuang

Th Atsadang

9

Wat Phra Kaew

3

Th Arun Amarin

Grand Palace

Th Sanam Chai

Th Ratchini

For reviews see

◉ Top Sights p24
◉ Sights p35
✕ Eating p37
🅖 Drinking p38
★ Entertainment p39

KO RATANAKOSIN

Saranrom Royal Garden

4

Mae Nam Chao Phraya

Th Charoen Krung

Khlong Mon

Tha Tien

Wat Pho

Museum of Siam

Th Arun Amarin

Th Wang Doem

Tha Wat Arun

Soi Pratu Nokyung

10

8

THONBURI

Wat Arun

11 6

Chetawan Traditional Massage School

Soi Pen Phat

1

5

National Museum

Sights

Museum of Siam
MUSEUM

1  Map p34, D5

This fun museum employs a variety
of methods and media to explore
the origins of the Thai people and
their culture. Housed in a European-
style 19th-century building that was
once the Ministry of Commerce, the
exhibits are presented in an engaging,
interactive fashion not typical of Thai
museums. A great option for those
travelling with kids.
(สถาบันพิพิธภัณฑ์การเรียนรู้แห่งชาติ; www.
museumsiam.com; Th Maha Rat; admission
300B; ☉10am-6pm Tue-Sun; ⚐; ⚑Tha
Tien)

National Museum
MUSEUM

2  Map p34, C2

Thailand's National Museum is
the largest in Southeast Asia and
covers a broad range of subjects,
from historical surveys to religious
sculpture displays. The buildings
were originally constructed in 1782 as
the palace of Rama I's viceroy, Prince
Wang Na. Rama V (King Chulalongkorn; r 1868–1910) turned it into a
museum in 1884. Free guided tours
are given on Wednesday and Thursday
at 9.30am.
(พิพิธภัณฑสถานแห่งชาติ; 4 Th Na Phra
That; admission 200B; ☉9am-4pm Wed-Sun;
⚑Tha Chang)

Top Tip

Dress for Success

Most of Bangkok's biggest tourist attractions are in fact sacred places, and visitors should dress and behave appropriately. In particular, at Wat Phra Kaew and the Grand Palace, you won't be allowed to enter unless you're well covered. Shorts, sleeveless shirts or spaghetti-strap tops, capri pants – basically anything that reveals more than your arms and head – are not allowed. Those who aren't dressed appropriately can expect to be shown into a dressing room and issued with a sarong before being allowed in.

Chetawan Traditional Massage School

MASSAGE

3 Map p34, C5

Stop by for a Thai-style massage, or if you've got more time, enrol in one of several reputable massage courses. The school is outside the Wat Pho temple compound in a restored Bangkok shophouse at the end of unmarked Soi Pen Phat; look for Coconut Palm restaurant. (✆ 0 2622 3551; www.watpomassage.com; 392/32-33 Soi Phen Phat; Thai massage per hour 420B, lessons from 2500B; ⏲8.30am-6pm; 🚤Tha Tien)

Songkran Niyomsane Forensic Medicine Museum & Parasite Museum

MUSEUM

4 ◎ Map p34, A2

Not for the faint of heart, pickled body parts, ingenious murder weapons and other bits of crime-scene evidence form the attractions at this macabre medical museum. Next door, the Parasite Museum continues the queasy theme. The best way to get here is by express ferry or cross-river ferry to Tha Wang Lang/Siriraj in Thonburi; turn right (north) into the hospital and follow the green 'Museum' signs. (พิพิธภัณฑ์นิติเวชศาสตร์สงกรานต์นิยมเสน; 2nd fl, Adulyadejvikrom Bldg, Siriraj Hospital; admission 200B; ⏲10am-4pm Wed-Mon; 🚤Tha Wang Lang/Siriraj)

Royal Barges National Museum

MUSEUM

5 ◎ Map p34, A1

For ceremonial occasions, the elaborately carved barges at this museum are dusted off for a grand riverine procession. The *Supphannahong* boat traditionally carries the king and is the world's largest dugout. Visit the museum as part of the long-tail boat tour of Thonburi, or from Tha Saphan Pin Klao, turn down Th Somdet Phra Pin Klao 1 and follow the signs. (พิพิธภัณฑสถานแห่งชาติ เรือพระราชพิธี/เรือพระที่นั่ง; Khlong Bangkok Noi or 80/1 Th Arun Amarin; admission 100B, camera 100B; ⏲9am-5pm; 🚤Tha Saphan Phra Pin Klao)

Eating

Coconut Palm
THAI **$**

6 Map p34, C5

Coconut Palm serves a generous spread of Thai dishes, but most locals come for the Sukhothai-style noodles – thin rice noodles served with pork, ground peanuts and dried chilli. Even if you're not hungry, you might want to stop by for the reinvigorating blast of air-con and the refreshing drinks.

(www.coconutpalmrestaurant.com; 392/1-2 Th Maha Rat; mains 40-100B; ☉11am-6pm; ❀Tha Tien)

Ming Lee
CHINESE-THAI **$**

7 Map p34, C3

Seemingly hidden in plain sight across from Wat Phra Kaew is this decades-old shophouse restaurant. The menu spans Western/Chinese dishes (such as stewed tongue) and Thai standards (such as the impossibly tart and garlicky 'beef spicy salad'). Often closed before 6pm, Ming Lee is best approached as a post-sightseeing lunch option. No roman-script sign.

(28-30 Th Na Phra Lan; mains 70-100B; ☉11.30am-6pm; ❀Tha Chang)

Pa Aew
CENTRAL THAI **$**

8 Map p34, C5

Yes, it's a bare-bones open-air curry stall, but if we're talking taste, Pa Aew is one of our favourite places to eat in this part of town. Pull up a plastic stool for rich, seafood-heavy Bangkok-style dishes. There's no sign here; look for the exposed trays of food directly in front of Krung Thai Bank.

(Th Maha Rat; mains 20-60B; ☉10am-5pm; ❀Tha Tien)

Khunkung
CENTRAL THAI **$$**

9 Map p34, B3

The restaurant of the Royal Navy Association has a coveted riverfront location along Mae Nam Chao Phraya.

Local Life
Exploring Thonburi's Canals

For an up-close view of Thonburi's famed canals, long-tail boats are available for charter at Tha Chang and Tha Tien from 8.30am to 5pm. Trips explore **Khlong Bangkok Noi** and **Khlong Bangkok Yai**, taking in the Royal Barges National Museum, Wat Arun and a riverside temple with fish feeding. Longer excursions make side trips into **Khlong Mon**, between Bangkok Noi and Bangkok Yai, and, on weekends, include a stop at the floating market at Taling Chan. However, it's worth pointing out that the most common tour of one hour (1000B, up to eight people) does not allow you enough time to disembark and explore any of these sights. To do so, you'll need 1½ hours (1300B) or two hours (1500B).

Locals come for the combination of breezy views and cheap and tasty seafood-based eats – not for the cafeteria-like atmosphere. Look for the sign on Th Maha Rat that says 'Navy Club'.

(Navy Club; 77 Th Maha Rat; mains 75-720B; ⏰11am-2pm & 6-10pm Mon-Fri, 11am-10pm Sat & Sun; 🛳Tha Chang)

Sala Rattanakosin   THAI $$$

10 🍴 Map p34, C5

Located on an open-air deck next to the river with Wat Arun virtually towering overhead, the Sala Rattanakosin hotel's signature restaurant has nailed the location. The food – largely central and northern Thai dishes with occasional Western twists – doesn't always live up to the scenery, but for upscale dining in this corner of town it's really the only option.

(📞0 2622 1388; www.salaresorts.com/rattanakosin; Sala Rattanakosin, 39 Th Maha Rat; mains 240-1100B; ⏰11am-4pm & 5.30-11pm; 🛳Tha Tien)

Drinking

Roof   BAR

The chic open-air bar on top of the new Sala Rattanakosin hotel (see 10 🍴 Map p34, C5) has upped the stakes for sunset views of Wat Arun – if you can

Amulet Market

LONELY PLANET / GETTY IMAGES ©

Local Life
Amulet Market

Bangkok's arcane and fascinating **amulet market** (ตลาดพระเครื่องวัด มหาธาตุ; Map p34, B2; Th Maha Rat; ☉7am-5pm; 🚢Tha Chang) claims the footpaths along Th Maha Rat and Th Phra Chan, as well as a dense network of covered market stalls near Tha Phra Chan. The trade is based around small talismans highly prized by collectors, monks, taxi drivers and people in dangerous professions.

see the temple at all through the wall of selfie-snapping tourists. (www.salaresorts.com/rattanakosin; rooftop, Sala Rattanakosin, 39 Th Maha Rat; ☉5pm-midnight Mon-Thu, to 1am Fri-Sun; 🚢Tha Tien)

Amorosa   BAR

11 Map p34, C5

Perched above the Arun Residence, Amorosa takes advantage of a location directly above the river and opposite Wat Arun. The cocktails aren't going to blow you away, but watching boats ply their way along the royal river as Wat Arun lights beyond is a touching reminder that you're not home any more.

(www.arunresidence.com; rooftop, Arun Residence, 36-38 Soi Pratu Nokyung; ☉5pm-midnight Mon-Thu, to 1am Fri-Sun; 🚢Tha Tien)

Entertainment

National Theatre   THEATRE

12 ⭐ Map p34, C1

After a lengthy renovation, the National Theatre is again open for business. Performances of *kŏhn*, masked dance-drama often depicting scenes from the *Ramakian*, are held on the first and second Sundays of the month; *lá·kon*, Thai dance-dramas, are held on the last Friday of the month; and Thai musical performances are held on the third Friday of the month.

(☎0 2224 1342; 2 Th Ratchini; tickets 60-100B; 🚢Tha Chang)

Explore

Banglamphu

Leafy lanes, antique shophouses, charming wet markets and golden temples convene in Banglamphu, easily the city's most quintessentially 'Bangkok' neighbourhood. It can appear to be a quaint postcard picture of the city that used to be – that is until you stumble upon Th Khao San, the intergalactic backpacker melting pot that's anything but traditional.

KAMPEE PATISENA / GETTY IMAGES ©

The Sights in a Day

☀ Start your day with a bird's-eye view of Banglamphu from the peak of the **Golden Mount** (p46). Descend and learn about the unique local trade at nearby **Ban Baat** (p46). Continue by foot to the impressive but little-visited **Wat Suthat** (p46).

☀ You're now a short walk from classic Bangkok-style restaurants **Krua Apsorn** (p49) and **Poj Spa Kar** (p53). After refuelling, cross over to Th Khao San, taking in the famous backpacker district's hectic **street market** (p57). Indulge in even more retail at niche shops **Nittaya Thai Curry** (p57) or **Taekee Taekon** (p57), or relax by the river at **Phra Sumen Fort & Santi Chai Prakan Park** (p46).

☾ Come evening, you have two options. If you're more of a spectator, consider dinner at **Likhit Kai Yang** (p49) followed by a few rounds of Thai boxing at **Ratchadamnoen Stadium** (p54); if you've got partying on the mind, hit the decadent noodles at **Jay Fai** (p49) followed by drinks with local hipsters at **Hippie de Bar** (p53) or **Phra Nakorn Bar & Gallery** (p53).

For a local's night in Banglamphu, see p42.

🔍 Local Life

Banglamphu Pub Crawl (p42)

💜 Best of Bangkok

Temples
Wat Suthat (p46)

Golden Mount & Wat Saket (p46)

Live Music
Brick Bar (p54)

Ad Here the 13th (p56)

Street Food
Jay Fai (p49)

Thip Samai (p50)

Ethnic Cuisine
Shoshana (p49)

Markets
Thanon Khao San Market (p57)

Rooftop Bars
Phra Nakorn Bar & Gallery (p53)

Dance Clubs
The Club (p53)

Getting There

🚢 **River ferry** Tha Phra Athit/Banglamphu.

🚢 **Klorng boat** Phanfa Leelard Pier.

Local Life
Banglamphu Pub Crawl

You don't need to go far to find a decent bar in Banglamphu – it's one of Bangkok's best nightlife 'hoods – but why limit yourself to one? With this in mind, we've assembled a pub crawl that spans river views, people-watching, live music and late-night shenanigans.

1 River Views

Begin your crawl in air-conditioned comfort at **Sheepshank** (📞0 2629 5165; www.sheepshankpublichouse.com; 47 Th Phra Athit; mains 320-1150B; ⏰6pm-midnight Tue-Sat; 🚤Tha Phra Athit/Banglamphu), a gastropub with bar snacks and classic cocktails, or *en plein air* at **Babble & Rum** (www.snhcollection.com/rivasurya; Riva Surya hotel, 23 Th Phra Athit; ⏰5-10pm; 🚤Tha Phra Athit/Banglamphu), the Riva Surya hotel's riverside restaurant-bar.

❷ People-Watching

Cross over to Soi Ram Buttri for phase two of your crawl. **Gecko Bar** (cnr Soi Chana Songkhram & Soi Rambutri; ⏱10am-1am; 🚤Tha Phra Athit/Banglamphu) is a cheap, low-key spot from which to gawk at passers-by, while a few doors down, **Madame Musur** (41 Soi Ram Buttri; ⏱8am-1am; 🚤Tha Phra Athit/Banglamphu) offers the same perks, but with a bit more sophistication and northern-style Thai dishes.

❸ Urban Beach

There seems to be a current (and inexplicable) trend for beach-themed, almost tiki-bar-style pubs in Banglamphu. If this aesthetic appeals, head south on Soi Ram Buttri and hunker down with a fruity cocktail among the Easter Island heads and bamboo decor at **Sawasdee House** (147 Soi Ram Buttri; ⏱11am-2am; 🚤Tha Phra Athit/Banglamphu) or, just south of Th Chakraphatdi Phong, the **Macaroni Club** (36 Th Rambuttri; ⏱24hr; 🚤Tha Phra Athit/Banglamphu).

❹ Live Music

Every pub crawl requires at least one singalong to a cheesy covers soundtrack (if you haven't yet heard a live version of 'Hotel California', you haven't really been to Bangkok), so continue along Th Rambuttri, stopping in at some of the numerous open-air live-music bars such as **Barlamphu** (Th Rambuttri; ⏱noon-1am; 🚤Tha Phra Athit/Banglamphu) or, 150m further south, **Molly Bar** (108 Th Rambuttri; ⏱8pm-1am; 🚤Tha Phra Athit/Banglamphu).

❺ Th Khao San

At this point, you should be sufficiently lubricated for the main event: Th Khao San. Get a bird's-eye view of the multinational backpacker parade from elevated **Roof Bar** (Th Khao San; ⏱5pm-midnight; 🚤Tha Phra Athit/Banglamphu) or from street level at the noisy and buzzy **Center Khao Sarn** (Th Khao San; ⏱24hr; 🚤Tha Phra Athit/Banglamphu), roughly across the street.

❻ Dance Fever

If you can muster the energy, it's probably the right time to hit one of Th Khao San's nightclubs such as **Lava Gold** (www.facebook.com/Lava.Gold.Club; 249 Th Khao San; admission free; ⏱7pm-4am; 🚤Tha Phra Athit/Banglamphu). Don't bother checking in before midnight.

❼ Late Night

If 2am (the closing time of most bars in the area) is too early for you to call it a night, crawl over to **Bank** (3rd fl, 44 Th Chakraphatdi Phong; ⏱6pm-late; 🚤Tha Phra Athit/Banglamphu), a rooftop lounge and nightclub that stays open late – very late. Don't say we didn't warn you...

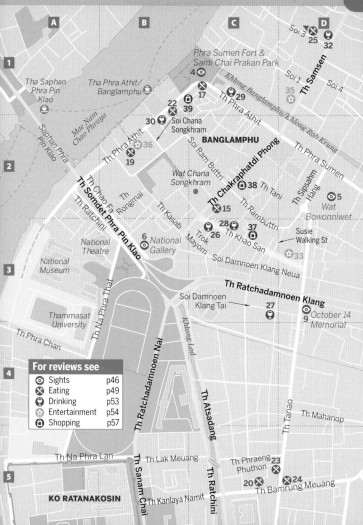

BANGLAMPHU

Phra Sumen Fort &
Santi Chai Prakan Park

Tha Saphan
Phra Pin
Klao

Tha Phra Athit/
Banglamphu

Mae Nam
Chao Phraya

Saphan Phra
Pin Klao

Th Phra Athit

Khlong Banglamphu/Khlong Rong Krung

Soi Chana
Songkhram

Th Phra Athit

Soi Ram Buttri

Wat Chana
Songkhram

Th Chakraphatdi Phong

Th Tani

Th Rambuttri

Th Khao San

Th Sipsahn
Hang

Wat
Bowonniwet

Susie
Walking St

Th Sondet Phra Pin Klao

Th Chao Fa

Th Rongmai

Th Kasab

Trok
Mayom

Th Ratchini

National
Theatre

National
Gallery

National
Museum

Soi Damnoen Klang Neua

Thammasat
University

Th Na Phra That

Th Ratchadamnoen Klang

Soi Damnoen
Klang Tai

October 14
Memorial

Th Phra Chan

Khlong Lod

Th Ratchadamnoen Nai

Th Atsadang

Th Tanao

Th Mahanop

For reviews see	
◉ Sights	p46
✖ Eating	p49
🅟 Drinking	p53
✪ Entertainment	p54
🄰 Shopping	p57

Th Na Phra Lan

Th Sanam Chai

Th Lak Meuang

Th Ratchini

KO RATANAKOSIN

Th Kanlaya Namit

Th Phraeng
Phuthon

Th Bamrung Meuang

Soi 3

Th Samsen

Soi 1

Soi 4

E   F   G   H

Th Wisut Kaset

Th Prachathipatai

Th Prachathipatai

Khlong Phadung Kasem

Th Krung Kasem

Th Prachathipatai

31

Th Prachathipatai

34 **14**

Tourism
Authority
of Thailand

Th Chakraphatdi Phong

21

Th Ratchadamnoen Nok

Th Din So

Th Phra Sumen

18

Th Nakhon Sawan

Th Ratchadamnoen Klang

Queen's
Gallery **10**

8 King Prajadhipok
Museum

Th Lan Luang

Th Din So

Ratchadamnoen
12 Contemporary
Art Center **11**

Phanfa Leelard Pier

Khlong Saen Saeb

Wat Ratchanatdaram **7**

Th Mahachai

Golden
1 Mount &
Wat Saket

Th Boriphat

Bangkok
City Hall

Th Mahanop

16

Sao Ching-Cha
(Giant Swing) **13**

Th Bamrung
Meuang

3 Ban Baat
Soi Ban Baat

Th Bamrung Meuang

2 Wat
Suthat

Sights

Golden Mount & Wat Saket
BUDDHIST TEMPLE

1 ◎ Map p44, G4

A less conspicuous stop on the temple itinerary, the Golden Mount is an artificial hill from which Bangkok appears meditatively serene. Next door, the enclosed *bòht* (ordination hall) of Wat Saket has some beautiful (and some gory) Buddhist murals. Join the candlelit procession to the summit in November during the annual temple fair.

(ภูเขาทอง, วัดสระเกศ; Th Boriphat; admission free; ⊘7.30am-5.30pm; ⛴klorng boat to Phanfa Leelard Pier)

Wat Suthat
BUDDHIST TEMPLE

2 ◎ Map p44, E5

Other than being just plain huge and impressive, Wat Suthat also holds the highest royal temple grade. Inside the *wí·hǎhn* (sanctuary for a Buddha sculpture) are intricate *Jataka* (stories of the Buddha) murals and Thailand's biggest surviving Sukhothai-era bronze Buddha. Over the road is **Sao Ching-Cha** (Giant Swing), site of a former Brahman festival in honour of Shiva.

(วัดสุทัศน์; Th Bamrung Meuang; admission 20B; ⊘8.30am-8.30pm; ⛴klorng boat to Phanfa Leelard Pier)

Ban Baat
NEIGHBOURHOOD

3 ◎ Map p44, F5

The residents of Ban Baat, the only surviving village of three founded by Rama I, still hand-hammer eight pieces of steel (representing Buddha's eightfold path) into the distinctive alms bowls used by monks to receive morning food donations. Tourists – not temples – are the primary customers these days, and a bowl purchase is usually rewarded with a demonstration.

(บ้านบาตร, Monk's Bowl Village; Soi Ban Baat; admission free; ⊘8am-5pm; ⛴klorng boat to Phanfa Leelard Pier)

Phra Sumen Fort & Santi Chai Prakan Park
NOTABLE BUILDING, PARK

4 ◎ Map p44, C1

Formerly the site of a sugar factory, today Santi Chai Prakan Park is a tiny patch of greenery with a great river view and lots of evening action, including comical communal aerobics classes. The riverside pathway heading southwards makes for a serene promenade. The park's most prominent landmark is the blindingly white Phra Sumen Fort, which was built in 1783 to defend the city against a river invasion.

(ป้อมพระสุเมรุ, สวนสันติชัยปราการ; Th Phra Athit; admission free; ⊘5am-9pm; ⛴Tha Phra Athit/Banglamphu)

Wat Suthat

Wat Bowonniwet
BUDDHIST TEMPLE

5 Map p44, D2

Home to the Buddhist Mahamakut University, this royally affiliated monastery is the national headquarters of the Thammayut sect of Thai Buddhism. The murals in the *bòht* are noteworthy, and include Thai depictions of Western life during the early 19th century. The temple may be in ultracasual Banglamphu, but it's also where the present king was ordained, so visitors must dress appropriately. (วัดบวรนิเวศวิหาร; www.watbowon.org; Th Phra Sumen; admission free; ⏲8.30am-5pm; 🚤Tha Phra Athit/Banglamphu)

National Gallery
ART GALLERY

6 Map p44, B3

Housed in a weathered colonial building that was the Royal Mint during the reign of Rama V, the National Gallery's permanent exhibition is admittedly a rather dusty and dated affair. More interesting are the rotating exhibits held in the spacious rear galleries; take a look at the posters out front to see what's on. (พิพิธภัณฑ์สถานแห่งชาติหอศิลป์/หอศิลป์ เจ้าฟ้า; ngbangkok.wordpress.com; 4 Th Chao Fa; admission 200B; ⏲9am-4pm Wed-Sun; 🚤Tha Phra Athit/Banglamphu)

Wat Ratchanatdaram
BUDDHIST TEMPLE

7 Map p44, F4

Built for Rama III (King Phranangklao; r 1824–51) in the 1840s, this temple's design is said to derive from metal temples built in India and Sri Lanka more than 2000 years ago. At the back of the compound is a well-known market selling Buddhist *prá krêu·ang* (amulets) in all sizes, shapes and styles.

(วัดราชนัดดาราม; Th Mahachai; admission free; ⊘8am-5pm; 🚤klorng boat to Phanfa Leelard Pier)

King Prajadhipok Museum
MUSEUM

8 Map p44, F4

This collection assembles old photos and other media to illustrate the rather dramatic life of Rama VII (King Prajadhipok; r 1925–35), Thailand's last absolute monarch. The museum occupies a grand neocolonial-style building constructed on the orders of Rama V for his favourite firm of Bond St merchants; it was the only foreign business allowed on the royal road linking Bangkok's two palace districts.

(พิพิธภัณฑ์พระบาทสมเด็จพระปกเกล้าเจ้าอยู่หัว; www.kingprajadhipokmuseum.org; 2 Th Lan Luang; admission free; ⊘9am-4pm Tue-Sun; 🚤klorng boat to Phanfa Leelard Pier)

October 14 Memorial
MONUMENT

9 Map p44, D3

A peaceful amphitheatre commemorates the civilian demonstrators who were killed by the military during a prodemocracy rally on 14 October 1973. More than 200,000 people had assembled at the adjacent Democracy Monument to protest against the arrest of political campaigners and continuing military dictatorship. Although some in Thailand continue to deny it, photographs confirm that more than 70 demonstrators were killed.

(อนุสรณ์สถาน ๑๔ ตุลา; cnr Th Ratchadamnoen Klang & Th Tanao; admission free; ⊘24hr; 🚤klorng boat to Phanfa Leelard Pier)

Queen's Gallery
ART GALLERY

10 Map p44, F4

This royal-funded museum presents five floors of rotating exhibitions of modern and traditionally influenced art. The building is sleek and contemporary and the artists hail from the upper echelons of the conservative Thai art world. The attached shop is filled with fine-arts books and gifts.

(www.queengallery.org; 101 Th Ratchadamnoen Klang; admission 30B; ⊘10am-7pm Thu-Tue; 🚤klorng boat to Phanfa Leelard Pier)

✓ Top Tip

Take the Boat

Traffic in Bangkok's old town can be brutal, and boats – both the Chao Phraya Express Boat and the *klorng* boats – are a steady, if slow, way to reach Banglamphu.

Ratchadamnoen Contemporary Art Center

ART GALLERY

11 Map p44, F4

Just opened at research time, this vast, three-storey structure is set to host changing exhibitions of mixed-media contemporary art by Thai and foreign artists. (RCAC; www.facebook.com/Ratchadamnone; Th Ratchadamnoen Klang; admission free; ⊙10am-7pm Tue-Sun; 🛥️klorng boat to Phanfa Leelard Pier)

Eating

Krua Apsorn

CENTRAL THAI $$

12 Map p44, E4

Patronised by royalty and lauded by the press, it's hard to think of a better intro to the flavours of Bangkok than this institution. Everything's tasty, but locals go crazy for the 'stir-fried crab with chili' and the decadent, *tortilla Española*–like 'omelet with crab'. (www.kruaapsorn.com; Th Din So; mains 70-400B; ⊙10.30am-8pm Mon-Sat; 🛥️klorng boat to Phanfa Leelard Pier)

Jay Fai

CENTRAL THAI $$$

13 Map p44, F5

You wouldn't think so by looking at her bare-bones dining room, but Jay Fai is known far and wide for serving Bangkok's most decadent – and expensive – *pàt kêe mow* (drunkard's noodles; wide rice noodles fried with

copious seafood and Thai herbs). Jay Fai doesn't have a roman-script sign, but is located directly across Th Mahachai from a 7-Eleven. (327 Th Mahachai; mains 180-1000B; ⊙3pm-2am Mon-Sat; 🛥️klorng boat to Phanfa Leelard Pier)

Likhit Kai Yang

NORTHEASTERN THAI $$

14 Map p44, G2

Located just behind Ratchadamnoen Stadium (avoid the rather grotty branch directly adjacent to the stadium), this decades-old restaurant is where locals come for a northeastern Thai–style meal before a Thai boxing match. The friendly English-speaking owner will coach you through the ordering process, but don't miss the deliciously herbal, eponymous 'charcoal roasted chicken'. There's no roman-script sign; look for the huge yellow banner. (off Th Ratchadamnoen Nok; mains 60-270B; ⊙9am-9pm; 🛥️klorng boat to Phanfa Leelard Pier)

Shoshana

ISRAELI $$

15 Map p44, C2

One of Khao San's longest-running Israeli restaurants, Shoshana resembles your grandparents' living room, right down to the tacky wall art and plastic placemats. Feel safe ordering anything deep-fried – they do an excellent job of it – and don't miss the deliciously garlicky eggplant dip.

(88 Th Chakraphatdi Phong; mains 70-240B; ⏰10am-midnight; 📶; 🚉Tha Phra Athit/ Banglamphu)

Thip Samai CENTRAL THAI $

16 Map p44, F5

Brace yourself, but you should be aware that the fried noodles sold from carts along Th Khao San have little to do with the dish known as *pàt tai*. Luckily, less than a five-minute túk-túk ride away lies Thip Samai, home to the most legendary Thai-style fried noodles in town. Closed on alternate Wednesdays.

(313 Th Mahachai; mains 50-250B; ⏰5pm-2am; 🚤klorng boat to Phanfa Leelard Pier)

Roti-Mataba MUSLIM-THAI $

17 Map p44, C1

This classic Bangkok eatery may have become a bit too big for its britches

in recent years, but it still serves tasty Thai-Muslim dishes such as roti, *gaang mát·sà·màn* (Muslim curry), a brilliantly sour fish curry, and *má·dà·bà* (a sort of stuffed Muslim-style pancake). An upstairs air-con dining area and outdoor tables provide additional seating for its loyal fans.

(136 Th Phra Athit; dishes 17-111B; ⏰9am-10pm Tue-Sun; 📶; 🚉Tha Phra Athit/ Banglamphu)

Seven Spoons INTERNATIONAL $$$

18 Map p44, G3

Dark woods, smooth concrete, a menu with influences ranging from Montreal to Morocco – one doesn't expect a place this modern and cosmopolitan in such an antiquated corner of Bangkok. Lots of vegetarian options.

(📞0 2629 9214, 08 4539 1819; sevenspoons-bkk.wordpress.com; 22-24 Th Chakraphatdi Phong; mains 160-580B; ⏰11am-3pm & 6pm-1am Tue-Sat, 6pm-1am Sun; 📶; 🚤klorng boat to Phanfa Leelard Pier)

Hemlock THAI $$

19 Map p44, B2

Taking full advantage of its cosy shophouse location, this perennial favourite has enough style to feel like a special night out, and doesn't skimp on flavour or preparation. The eclectic menu reads like an ancient literary work, reviving old dishes from aristocratic kitchens across the country.

(56 Th Phra Athit; mains 75-280B; ⏰4pm-midnight Mon-Sat; 📶; 🚉Tha Phra Athit/ Banglamphu)

✅ Top Tip

What's Your Name?

Banglamphu means 'Place of Lamphu', a reference to the *lam·poo* tree (*Duabanga grandiflora*) that was once prevalent in the area; the last remaining one can be found at Santi Chai Prakan Park (p46).

Understand

Thanon Khao San

Th Khao San, better known as Khao San Rd, is unlike anywhere else on earth. It's a clearing house of people either entering the liberated state of travelling in Southeast Asia or returning to the coddling bonds of first-world life, all coming together in a neon-lit melting pot in Banglamphu. Its uniqueness is best illustrated by a question: apart from airports, where else could you share space with the citizens of dozens of countries, people ranging from first-time backpackers scoffing banana pancakes to 75-year-old grandparents ordering G&Ts, and everyone in between?

The Emergence of an Icon

Th Khao San (*cow-sarn*), meaning 'uncooked rice', is perhaps the highest-profile bastard child of the age of independent travel. Of course, it hasn't always been this way. For its first two centuries it was just an unremarkable road in old Bangkok. The first guesthouses appeared in 1982, and as more backpackers arrived through the '80s, the old wooden homes were converted one by one into low-rent dosshouses. By the time Alex Garland's novel *The Beach* was published in 1997, with its opening scenes set on the seedier side of Khao San, staying here had become a rite of passage for backpackers coming to Southeast Asia.

The Khao San of Today

Publicity from Garland's book and the movie that followed pushed Khao San into the mainstream, romanticising the seediness, and stereotyping the backpackers it attracted as unwashed and counterculturalist. It also brought the long-simmering debate about the relative merits of Th Khao San to the top of backpacker conversations. Was it cool to stay on KSR? Was it uncool? Was this 'real travel' or just an international anywhere surviving on the few baht Western backpackers spent before they headed home to start high-earning careers? Was it really Thailand at all? Perceptions aside, today the strip continues to anticipate every traveller's need: meals to soothe homesickness, cafes and bars for swapping travel tales, tailors, travel agents, teeth whitening, secondhand books, hair braiding and, of course, the perennial Akha women trying to harass everyone they see into buying those croaking wooden frogs.

Vegging Out in Banglamphu

Due to the strong foreign influence, there's an abundance of vegetarian restaurants in the Banglamphu area. In addition to Hemlock (p50) and Shoshana (p49), both of which have generous meat-free sections, vegetarian alternatives include the following:

Arawy Vegetarian Food (Map p44, E4; 152 Th Din So; mains 20-40B; ⊙7am-8.30pm; 🍽; 🚣klorng boat to Phanfa Leelard Pier) Heaps of prepared meat-free curries, dips and stir-fries.

Thamna (175 Th Samsen; mains 90-190B; ⊙11am-3pm & 5-9pm Mon-Sat; 🍽; 🚣Tha Phra Athit/Banglamphu) Fusiony vegetarian dishes that will make even the meat-eaters smile.

May Kaidee's (Map p44, D1; www.maykaidee.com; 33 Th Samsen; mains 50-100B; ⊙9am-10pm; 🍽; 🚣Tha Phra Athit/Banglamphu) A long-standing restaurant that also houses a veggie Thai cooking school.

Nuttaporn
THAI $

20 🍽 Map p44, C5

A crumbling shophouse that for the last 70 years has been churning Bangkok's most famous coconut ice cream – in our opinion the idea palate cleanser after a bowl of spicy Thai noodles.

(94 Th Phraeng Phuthon; mains from 20B; ⊙9am-4pm Mon-Sat; 🍽; 🚣Tha Phra Athit/Banglamphu)

Nang Loeng Market
THAI $

21 🍽 Map p44, H3

Dating back to 1899, this atmospheric fresh market offers a charming glimpse of old Bangkok, not to mention some tasty Thai-style curries and sweets.

(btwn Soi 8-10, Th Nakhon Sawan; mains 30-80B; ⊙10am-2pm Mon-Fri; 🚣klorng boat to Phanfa Leelard Pier)

Escapade Burgers & Shakes
AMERICAN $$

22 🍽 Map p44, B1

Escapade is proof that, when it comes to American food, the Thais have moved way beyond McDonald's. Squeeze into this tiny shophouse for messy burgers with edgy ingredients such as 'toasted rice mayo', and some pretty decadent milkshakes.

(112 Th Phra Athit; mains 120-330B; ⊙4pm-midnight Tue-Sun; 🚣Tha Phra Athit/Banglamphu)

Chote Chitr
CENTRAL THAI $

23 🍽 Map p44, C5

This third-generation shophouse restaurant boasting just six tables is a Bangkok foodie landmark. The kitchen can be inconsistent and the service consistently grumpy, but when they're on, dishes like *mèe gròrp* (crispy fried noodles) and *yam tòo·a ploo* (wing-bean salad) are in a class of their own.

(146 Th Phraeng Phuthon; mains 30-200B; ⊙11am-10pm; 🚣klorng boat to Phanfa Leelard Pier)

Poj Spa Kar

CENTRAL THAI $$

24 Map p44, D5

Pronounced *pôht sà·pah kahn*, this is allegedly the oldest restaurant in Bangkok, and continues to maintain recipes handed down from a former palace cook. Be sure to order the simple but tasty lemongrass omelette or the deliciously sour-sweet *gaang sôm*, a traditional central Thai soup. (443 Th Tanao; mains 65-200B; ⏱12.30-8.30pm; ⛴klorng boat to Phanfa Leelard Pier)

Khinlom Chom Sa-Phan

THAI $$

25 Map p44, D1

Locals come here for the combination of river views and tasty, seafood-based eats. It's popular, so be sure to call ahead if you want a riverside table. (☎0 2628 8382; www.khinlomchomsaphan. com; 11/6 Soi 3, Th Samsen; mains 75-280B; ⏱11am-2am; ⛴Tha Phra Athit/Banglamphu)

Drinking

Hippie de Bar

BAR

26 Map p44, C3

Our vote for Banglamphu's best bar, Hippie boasts a funky retro vibe and indoor and outdoor seating, all set to an indie/pop soundtrack that you're unlikely to hear elsewhere in town. Despite being located on Th Khao San, there are surprisingly few foreign faces, and it's a great place to make some new Thai friends.

(www.facebook.com/hippie.debar; 46 Th Khao San; ⏱3pm-2am; ⛴Tha Phra Athit/Banglamphu)

Phra Nakorn Bar & Gallery

BAR

27 Map p44, C3

Located an ambivalent arm's length from the hype of Th Khao San, Phra Nakorn Bar is a home away from hovel for students and arty types, with eclectic decor and changing gallery exhibits. Our tip: head directly for the breezy rooftop and order some of the bar's cheap 'n' tasty Thai food. (www.facebook.com/Phranakornbarandgallery; 58/2 Soi Damnoen Klang Tai; ⏱6pm-1am; ⛴klorng boat to Phanfa Leelard Pier)

The Club

CLUB

28 Map p44, C3

Located right in the middle of Th Khao San, this cavernlike dance hall hosts a good mix of locals and backpackers. Expect a door fee of 120B on Friday and Saturday nights. (www.theclubkhaosan.com; 123 Th Khao San; ⏱10pm-2am; ⛴Tha Phra Athit/Banglamphu)

Jham Jun

BAR

29 Map p44, C1

Boasting a rooftop address, a casual, loungey vibe, live music and an emphasis on food, Jham Jun is a characteristically Thai-style drinking spot a short walk from Th Khao San. (rooftop, Fortville Guesthouse, 9 Th Phra Athit; ⏱6pm-1am; ⛴Tha Phra Athit/Banglamphu)

Commé
BAR

30 Map p44, B2

The knot of vintage motorcycles is your visual cue, but most likely you'll hear Commé before you see it. A staple for local hipsters, this classic Th Phra Athit–style semi-open-air bar is the place to go for a loud, boozy, Thai-style night out.

(100/4-5 Th Phra Athit; ⏰6pm-1am; 🚤Tha Phra Athit/Banglamphu)

Rolling Bar
BAR

31 Map p44, E2

An escape from hectic Th Khao San is a good-enough excuse to schlep to this quiet canal-side boozer. Live music and salty bar snacks are good reasons to stay.

(Th Prachathipatai; ⏰5pm-midnight; 🚤klorng boat to Phanfa Leelard Pier)

Post Bar
BAR

32 Map p44, D1

If 'Chinese pawn shop' can be considered a legitimate design theme,

Post Bar has nailed it. The walls of this narrow, shophouse-bound bar are decked with retro Thai kitsch; the soundtrack is appropriately classic rock; and the clientele is overwhelmingly Thai.

(161 Th Samsen; ⏰7pm-1am; 🚤Tha Phra Athit/Banglamphu)

Entertainment

Brick Bar
LIVE MUSIC

33 ⭐ Map p44, D3

This basement pub, one of our fave destinations in Bangkok for live music, hosts a nightly revolving cast of Thai bands for an almost 100% Thai crowd, many of whom will end the night dancing on the tables. Brick Bar can get infamously packed, so be sure to get there early if you want a table.

(www.brickbarkhaosan.com; basement, Buddy Lodge, 265 Th Khao San; admission 150B Sat-Sun; ⏰7pm-2am; 🚤Tha Phra Athit/Banglamphu)

Ratchadamnoen Stadium
THAI BOXING

34 ⭐ Map p44, G2

Ratchadamnoen Stadium, Bangkok's oldest and most venerable venue for *moo·ay tai* (Thai boxing; also spelt *muay thai*) hosts matches on Monday, Wednesday, Thursday and Sunday starting at 6.30pm. Be sure to buy tickets from the official ticket counter,

---

Local Life
Off the Beaten Track

Although Th Khao San remains associated with foreign tourists, in recent years it's also become a popular nightlife destination for young locals. For an almost entirely local drinking scene, check out the live-music pubs along Th Phra Athit.

Understand
Thai Boxing

More formally known as Phahuyut (from the Pali-Sanskrit *bhahu*, meaning 'arm', and *yodha*, 'combat'), Thailand's ancient martial art of *moo·ay tai* (Thai boxing; also spelt *muay thai*) is one of the kingdom's most striking national icons.

An Ancient Tradition

Many martial-arts aficionados agree that *moo·ay tai* is the most efficient, effective and generally unbeatable form of ring-centred, hand-to-hand combat practised today. After the Siamese were defeated at Ayuthaya in 1767, several expert *moo·ay boh·rahn* (from which contemporary *moo·ay tai* is derived) fighters were among the prisoners hauled off to Burma. A few years later a festival was held; one of the Thai fighters, Nai Khanom Tom, was ordered to take on prominent Burmese boxers for the entertainment of the king and to determine which martial art was most effective. He promptly dispatched nine opponents in a row and, as legend has it, was offered money or beautiful women as a reward; he promptly took two new wives.

The Modern Game

In the early days of the sport, combatants' fists were wrapped in thick horsehide for maximum impact with minimum knuckle damage; tree bark and seashells were used to protect the groin from lethal kicks. But the high incidence of death and physical injury led the Thai government to ban *moo·ay tai* in the 1920s; in the 1930s the sport was revived under a modern set of regulations. Bouts were limited to five three-minute rounds separated by two-minute breaks. Contestants had to wear international-style gloves and trunks and their feet were taped – to this day no shoes are worn. In spite of all these concessions to safety, today all surfaces of the body remain fair targets and any part of the body except the head may be used to strike an opponent. Common blows include high kicks to the neck, elbow thrusts to the face and head, knee hooks to the ribs and low kicks to the calf. Punching is considered the weakest of all blows, and kicking merely a way to 'soften up' one's opponent; knee and elbow strikes are decisive in most matches.

Thanon Khao San (Khao San Rd; p51)

not from the touts who hang around outside the entrance.

(off Th Ratchadamnoen Nok; tickets 3rd-class/2nd-class/ringside 1000/1500/2000B; 🚣klorng boat to Phanfa Leelard Pier)

Ad Here the 13th
LIVE MUSIC

35 ⭐ Map p44, D1

Located beside Khlong Banglam-phu/Khlong Rob Krung, Ad Here is everything a neighbourhood joint should be: lots of regulars, cold beer and heart-warming tunes delivered by a masterful house band starting at 10pm. Everyone knows each other, so don't be shy about mingling.

(www.facebook.com/pages/Adhere-13th-blues-bar/97360378333; 13 Th Samsen;

🕑6pm-midnight; 🚣Tha Phra Athit/ Banglamphu)

jazz happens!
LIVE MUSIC

36 ⭐ Map p44, B2

Linked with Thailand's most famous arts university, jazz happens! is a stage for aspiring musical talent. With four acts playing most nights and a huge selection of bar snacks, you'll be thoroughly entertained.

(www.facebook.com/JazzHappens; 62 Th Phra Athit; 🕑7pm-1am; 🛜; 🚣Tha Phra Athit/ Banglamphu)

Shopping

Thanon Khao San Market

SOUVENIRS

37 Map p44, C3

The main guesthouse strip in Banglamphu is a day-and-night shopping bazaar, selling all but the baby and the bathwater. Cheap T-shirts, trendy purses, wooden frogs, fuzzy puppets, bootleg CDs, hemp clothing, fake student ID cards, knock-off designer wear, souvenirs, corn on the cob, orange juice... You name it, they've got it.

(Th Khao San; ⏱10am-midnight; 🚣Tha Phra Athit/Banglamphu)

Nittaya Thai Curry

FOOD & DRINK

38 Map p44, C2

Follow your nose: Nittaya is famous throughout Thailand for her pungent, high-quality curry pastes. Pick up a couple of takeaway canisters for prospective dinner parties or peruse the snack and gift sections, where visitors to Bangkok load up on local specialities for friends back in the provinces.

(136-40 Th Chakraphatdi Phong; ⏱9am-7pm Mon-Sat; 🚣Tha Phra Athit/Banglamphu)

Local Life

Buy-a-Buddha

The stretch of **Thanon Bamrung Meuang** (Map p44, E5) – one of Bangkok's oldest streets and originally an elephant path leading to the Grand Palace – from Th Mahachai to Th Tanao is lined with shops selling all manner of Buddhist religious paraphernalia. Behind the shopfronts, back-room workshops produce gigantic bronze Buddha images for wát all over Thailand. You probably don't need a Buddha statue or an eerily lifelike model of a famous monk, but looking is fun, and who knows when you might need to do a great deal of Thai-style merit making.

Taekee Taekon

HANDICRAFTS

39 Map p44, B1

This atmospheric shop has a decent selection of Thai textiles from the country's main silk-producing areas, especially northern Thailand, as well as assorted local knick-knacks and interesting postcards not generally available elsewhere.

(118 Th Phra Athit; ⏱9am-6pm Mon-Sat; 🚣Tha Phra Athit/Banglamphu)

Top Sights
Dusit Palace Park

Getting There

S **BTS** Phaya Thai exit 2 and taxi

⚓ **River ferry** Tha Thewet

Following his first European tour in 1897, Rama V (King Chulalongkorn; r 1868–1910) returned home with visions of European castles and set about transforming those styles into a uniquely Thai expression, today's Dusit Palace Park. The royal palace, throne hall and minor palaces for extended family were all moved here, and were supplemented with beaux-arts institutions and Victorian manor houses. The resulting fascinating architectural mishmash and the expansive gardens make the compound a worthwhile escape from the chaos of modern Bangkok.

Vimanmek Teak Mansion

Don't Miss

Vimanmek Teak Mansion

Originally constructed on Ko Si Chang in 1868 and moved to the present site in 1910, Vimanmek Teak Mansion contains 81 rooms, halls and anterooms, and is said to be the world's largest golden-teak building, allegedly built without the use of a single nail. Compulsory tours (in English) leave every half-hour between 9.45am and 3.15pm, and last about an hour.

Abhisek Dusit Throne Hall

Moorish palaces and Victorian mansions are the main influences on this intricate building of porticoes and fretwork fused with a distinctive Thai character. Today, the hall displays regional handiwork crafted by members of the Promotion of Supplementary Occupations & Related Techniques (Support), a charity foundation sponsored by Queen Sirikit.

Royal Elephant Museum

Near the Th U Thong Nai entrance are two stables that once housed three white elephants – their auspicious albinism automatically make such animals crown property. One of the structures contains artefacts outlining the importance of elephants in Thai history and explaining their various rankings according to physical characteristics. The second stable holds a sculptural representation of a living royal white elephant.

Other Exhibits

Near the Th Ratchawithi entrance, two residence halls display the **HM King Bhumibol Photography Exhibitions**, a collection of photographs and paintings by the present monarch. The **Ancient Cloth Museum** presents a beautiful collection of traditional silks and cottons.

วังสวนดุสิต

☎ 0 2628 6300

bounded by Th Ratchawithi, Th U Thong Nai & Th Ratchasima

adult/child 100/20B, or free with Grand Palace ticket

🕙 9.30am-4pm Tue-Sun

☑ Top Tips

▶ Entry is free if you're holding a same-day ticket from Wat Phra Kaew & Grand Palace (p24).

▶ Visitors should wear long trousers (no capri pants) or skirts and sleeved shirts.

✕ Take a Break

For a great-value riverside lunch, try **Kaloang Home Kitchen** (Th Si Ayuthaya; mains 60-170B; 🕙 11am-11pm; 🚢 Tha Thewet). Alternatively, make the short walk to a branch of the award-winning Thai restaurant **Krua Apsorn** (www.kruaapsorn.com; 503-505 Th Samsen; mains 65-350B; 🕙 10.30am-7.30pm Mon-Fri, to 6pm Sat; ❄; 🚢 Tha Thewet).

Explore

Chinatown

Although many generations removed from the mainland, Bangkok's Chinatown could be a bosom brother of any Chinese city. The streets are crammed with noodle and dim-sum restaurants, gaudy yellow-gold and jade shops, and flashing neon signs with Chinese characters. It's Bangkok's most hectic neighbourhood, and a great place in which to lose yourself in the crowd.

LONELY PLANET / GETTY IMAGES ©

The Sights in a Day

☼ Start your day early by beating the tour buses to the immense golden Buddha at **Wat Traimit** (p62). Continue, crossing through the frenetic market alleyway that is **Talat Mai** (p67), to the mazelike Chinese-style temple, **Wat Mangkon Kamalawat** (p68).

☼ Make your way – by foot or taxi – to **Phahurat** (p68), Bangkok's Little India. Take lunch at **Royal India** (p73) and, if you've got the space, a postlunch dessert at **Old Siam Plaza** (p72).

☾ Chinatown begins to pick up again in the early evening, and this is the best time to return to the area and follow our food-centric walking tour. After dinner, enjoy stunning views of Mae Nam Chao Phraya from the rooftop bar at **River Vibe** (p73). When it's as late as you're willing to stay up, cross over to the nocturnal flower market at **Pak Khlong Talat** (p67).

For a local's evening feasting in Chinatown, see p64.

◉ Top Sights

Wat Traimit (Golden Buddha; p62)

◯ Local Life

A Taste of Chinatown (p64)

♥ Best of Bangkok

Temples
Wat Traimit (Golden Buddha; p62)

Wat Mangkon Kamalawat (p68)

Street Food
Khun Yah Cuisine (p72)

Nay Hong (p72)

Nai Mong Hoi Thod (p64)

Th Phadungdao Seafood Stalls (p65)

Jék Pûi (p65)

Mangkorn Khŏw (p65)

Markets
Pak Khlong Talat (p67)

Talat Mai (p67)

Getting There

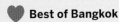

Ⓜ **MRT** Hua Lamphong.

⛴ **River ferry** Tha Marine Department, Tha Ratchawong and Tha Saphan Phut/Memorial Bridge.

Top Sights
Wat Traimit (Golden Buddha)

Wat Traimit, also known as the Temple of the Golden Buddha, is home to the world's largest gold statue, a gleaming, 3m-tall, 5.5-ton Buddha image with a mysterious past and a current value of more than US$250 million. Sculpted in the graceful Sukhothai style, the image is thought to date from as long ago as the 13th century, but if it is possible for a Buddha image to lead a double life, then this piece has most certainly done so.

วัด ไตรมิตร, Temple of the Golden Buddha

⊙ Map p66, D3

Th Mitthaphap/
Th Traimit

admission 40B

🕗 8am-5pm

⛴ Tha Ratchawong,
Ⓜ Hua Lamphong exit 1

Don't Miss

Golden Buddha

The star attraction at Wat Traimit is the gold Buddha image. Located on the 4th floor of the temple compound's imposing marble structure, the gold statue was originally 'discovered' some 60 years ago beneath a stucco or plaster exterior when it fell from a crane while being moved. It's thought that the covering was added to protect the statue from marauding hordes.

Phra Maha Mondop

In 2009 a new home for the Buddha statue was built. Combining marble, Chinese-style balustrades and a steep Thai-style roof, it's now one of the taller buildings in Chinatown, and the golden spire can be seen from blocks away. Surrounding the structure is a narrow strip of grass watered via mist fountains, and the usual Thai temple buildings.

Yaowarat Chinatown Heritage Center

On the 2nd floor of Phra Maha Mondop is this small but engaging **museum** (admission 100B; ⊘8am-5pm Tue-Sun), which houses multimedia exhibits on Chinese immigration to Thailand, as well as on the history of Bangkok's Chinatown and its residents. Particularly fun are the miniature dioramas that depict important cultural facets of Thai-Chinese life.

Phra Buddha Maha Suwanna Patimakorn Exhibition

An extension of the Yaowarat Chinatown Heritage Center, this 3rd-floor **exhibition** recounts how Wat Traimit's Buddha statue was made, discovered and transported to its current home. If you've ever wondered how to make – or move – a 5.5-ton gold Buddha statue, your questions will be answered here.

☑ **Top Tips**

▶ Wat Traimit is a short walk from the MRT stop at Hua Lamphong.

▶ Don't overlook the two interesting museums – closed on Mondays – located in the same structure as the Golden Buddha.

✗ **Take a Break**

Located in the same compound, in an un-signed covered structure just east of the Buddha statue, unassuming Khun Yah Cuisine (p72) does excellent central Thai–style curry and noodle dishes. There's no menu, rather just point to whatever looks tasty, and be sure to get there before noon.

Local Life
A Taste of Chinatown

Street food rules in Chinatown, making the area ideal for a culinary adventure. Although many vendors stay open late, the more popular stalls tend to sell out quickly, so the best time to feast in this area is from 7pm to 9pm. Don't attempt this walk on a Monday, when most of the city's street vendors stay at home. And note that many of the stalls don't have roman-script signs.

❶ Nai Mong Hoi Thod

Start at the intersection of Th Plaeng Nam and Th Charoen Krung. Head north along Th Phlap Phla Chai until you reach **Nai Mong Hoi Thod** (539 Th Phlap Phla Chai; mains 50-70B; ☺5-10pm Tue-Sun; ⛴Tha Ratchawong, ⓂHua Lamphong exit 1 & taxi), renowned for its delicious *or sòo·an* (mussels or oysters fried with egg and a sticky batter).

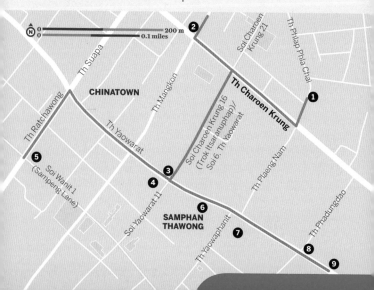

❷ Jék Pûi

Backtrack to Th Charoen Krung and turn right. Upon reaching Th Mangkon make a right. To your left is **Jék Pûi** (เจ็ก ปุ้ย; Th Mangkorn; mains from 30B; ⏰ 4-8pm Tue-Sun; 🚤 Tha Ratchawong, Ⓜ Hua Lamphong exit 1 & taxi), a tableless stall renowned for its mild Chinese-style Thai curries.

❸ Gŏo·ay đĕe·o kôo·a gài

Cross Th Charoen Krung again, turn left, and head east to Soi 16 (aka Trok Itsaranuphap). At the end of this narrow market lane you'll see a gentleman making **gŏo·ay đĕe·o kôo·a gài** (Soi 6, Th Yaowarat; mains from 30B; ⏰ 5-10pm Tue-Sun; 🚤 Tha Ratchawong, Ⓜ Hua Lamphong exit 1 & taxi), wide rice noodles fried with chicken, egg and garlic oil.

❹ Nay Lék Ûan

Upon emerging at Th Yaowarat, cross over to the market area across the street. The first vendor on the right, **Nay Lék Ûan** (นายเล็กอ้วน; Soi Yaowarat 11; mains from 40B; ⏰ 5pm-midnight; 🚤 Tha Ratchawong, Ⓜ Hua Lamphong exit 1 & taxi), sells *gŏo·ay jáp nám săi*, a peppery broth containing roll-like rice noodles and pork offal.

❺ Phat Thai Ratchawong

Go west on Th Yaowarat. Turn left onto Th Ratchawong, where **Phat Thai Ratchawong** (Th Ratchawong; mains from 30B; ⏰ 7-11pm Tue-Sun; 🚤 Tha Ratchawong, Ⓜ Hua Lamphong exit 1 & taxi), a stall run by a Chinese-Thai couple, offers a unique version of *pàt tai* – Thailand's most famous dish – fried over coals and served in banana-leaf cups.

❻ Mangkorn Khŏw

Backtrack along Th Yaowarat to the corner of Th Yaowaphanit, where you'll see **Mangkorn Khŏw** (cnr Th Yaowarat & Th Yaowaphanit; mains from 40B; ⏰ 5-11pm Tue-Sun; 🚤 Tha Ratchawong, Ⓜ Hua Lamphong exit 1 & taxi), a street stall selling tasty *bà·mèe*, Chinese-style wheat noodles served with crab or barbecued pork.

❼ Boo·a loy nám kĭng

Adjacent to Mangkorn Khŏw is a no-name stall that does Chinese-Thai desserts, including delicious **boo·a loy nám kĭng** (cnr Th Yaowarat & Th Yaowaphanit; mains from 30B; ⏰ 5-11pm Tue-Sun; 🖊; 🚤 Tha Ratchawong, Ⓜ Hua Lamphong exit 1 & taxi), dumplings stuffed with black sesame paste and served in a ginger broth.

❽ Th Phadungdao Seafood Stalls

Cross Th Yaowarat and head east until you reach the intersection with Th Phadungdao; this corner is the location of **Lek & Rut and T&K** (cnr Th Phadungdao & Th Yaowarat; mains 100-600B; ⏰ 4pm-midnight Tue-Sun; 🚤 Tha Ratchawong, Ⓜ Hua Lamphong exit 1 & taxi), two popular and nearly identical seafood stalls.

❾ Cotton

Continue east along Th Yaowarat until you reach the Shanghai Mansion hotel; on the 2nd floor here is **Cotton** (www.cotton.shanghaimansion.com; 2nd fl, Shanghai Mansion, 479-481 Th Yaowarat; ⏰ live music 6.30-10.30pm; 🚤 Tha Ratchawong, Ⓜ Hua Lamphong exit 1 & taxi), a jazz bar that's a timely – and graciously air-conditioned – end to your walk.

400 m
0.2 miles

Th Yukhol 2

Th Krung Kasem

Th Phra Ram IV

Hualamphong
Tram Station

Hua Lamphong

Th Luang

Th Mittaphan

Flashlight Market

Th Maitrichit

Wong Wian 22 Karakada

Soi Nana

Th Mittaphap (Th Traimit)

Th Charoen Krung

Soi Charoen Pranit

Th Suapa

Th Pinap Phla Chai

Th Mangkon

Santiphap

Th Plaeng Nam

Wat Traimit (Golden Buddha)

Soi Wanit 2

Th Yotha

Th Charoen Krung

Talat Noi

Th Maitrichit

Th Wat Mangkon Kamalawat

Soi Charoen Krung 16 (Trok Itsaranuphap)/ Soi 6, Th Yaowarat

Talat Mai

Th Charoen Krung

Soi Phanurangsi

Soi Phanurangsi

Th Luang

Th Maitrichit

Th Charoen Krung

Wat Patumkongka Rachaworawiham

Th Songwat

Soi Khang Wat Pathom Khongkha

Tha Marine Department

Th Chiangmai

Corrections Museum

Th Mahachai

Th Yaowarat

Sampeng Lane

Soi Wanit 1 (Sampeng Lane)

CHINATOWN

Th Ratchawong

Th Ratchawong

Tha Ratchawong

Mae Nam Chao Phraya

For reviews see

◎ Top Sights p62
◎ Sights p67
⊗ Eating p72
◯ Drinking p73
◐ Entertainment p75

Th Chakrawat

Gurdwara Siri Guru Singh Sabha

Th Burapha

Th Phahurat

Th Chakraphet

Saphan Phut Night Bazaar

Saphan Phut (Memorial Bridge)

Phra Pokklao Bridge

Th Charoen Krung

Th Triphet

Th Ban Mo

Pak Khlong Talat

Tha Pak Talat/ Atsadang

Saphan Phut/ Memorial Bridge

Church of Santa Cruz

Th Somdet Chao Phraya

Th Prachathipok

Saranrom Royal Garden

IGOR BILIC / GETTY IMAGES ©

Pak Khlong Talat

Sights

Pak Khlong Talat

MARKET

1 ◉ Map p66, A2

Come to this wholesale flower market late at night when shirtless porters wheeling mounds of orchids, piles of roses and stacks of button carnations set the place in motion. At press time, the indoor section of the market was being renovated, but the outside portion appeared unaffected.

(ปากคลองตลาด, Flower Market; Th Chakraphet; ⏱24hr; 🚤Tha Saphan Phut/Memorial Bridge)

Talat Mai

MARKET

2 ◉ Map p66, C2

Nudge your way deep into one of Chinatown's most famous capillaries, where vendors sell dried goods, half-alive filleted fish and vats of unidentifiable pickled stuff – among other exotic Chinese ingredients. The soi's poetic finale (north of Th Charoen Krung) is lined with stalls selling elaborate funeral offerings and 'passports to heaven', which include paper iPhones and cars to accompany deceased loved ones into the next life.

(ตลาดใหม่; Soi Charoen Krung 16/Trok Itsaranuphap/Soi 6, Th Yaowarat; ⏱6am-7pm; 🚤Tha Ratchawong, Ⓜ Hua Lamphong exit 1 & taxi)

Local Life

Living on a Prayer

In many of Chinatown's temples, you'll see locals shaking cans of thin sticks called *see·am see*. You can also play: when a stick falls to the floor, look at its number and find the corresponding paper. It will give you a no-nonsense appraisal of your future in Thai, Chinese and English.

Wat Mangkon Kamalawat

BUDDHIST TEMPLE

3 Map p66, D2

Explore the cryptlike sermon halls of this busy, recently renovated Chinese temple to find Buddhist, Taoist and Confucian shrines. During the annual Vegetarian Festival (p73), religious and culinary activities are centred here. But almost any time of day or night this temple is busy with worshippers lighting incense, filling the ever-burning altar lamps with oil and making offerings to their ancestors. (วัดมังกรกมลาวาส; cnr Th Charoen Krung & Th Mangkon; admission free; ⏰6am-6pm; 🚤Tha Ratchawong, Ⓜ Hua Lamphong exit 1 & taxi)

Flashlight Market

MARKET

4 Map p66, D1

This street market extends west from the Phlap Phla Chai intersection, forging a trail of antiques, secondhand items and, well, sometimes just plain junk, along the area's footpaths. It's at its busiest on Saturday night, when a flashlight is needed to see many of the goods for sale. (ตลาดไฟฉาย; cnr Th Phlap Phla Chai & Th Luang; ⏰5am Sat-5pm Sun; 🚤Tha Ratchawong, Ⓜ Hua Lamphong exit 1 & taxi)

Phahurat

NEIGHBOURHOOD

5 Map p66, B2

Heaps of South Asian traders set up shop in Bangkok's small but bustling Little India, where everything from Bollywood movies to Punjabi sweets is sold by small-time traders. Most of the action unfolds along the unmarked soi adjacent to the India Emporium mall. Phahurat is also associated with cloth, and its markets proffer flamboyant Bollywood-coloured textiles, traditional Thai dance costumes, tiaras, sequins, wigs and other accessories. (พาหุรัด; Th Chakraphet; ⏰9am-5pm; 🚤Tha Saphan Phut/Memorial Bridge)

Talat Noi

NEIGHBOURHOOD

6 Map p66, D4

This microcosm of soi life is named after a small (*nóy*) market that sets up along Soi Wanit 2, between Th Yotha and Soi Phanurangsi. Wandering here you'll find streamlike lanes turning in on themselves, weaving through people's living rooms, Chinese temples, noodle shops and grease-stained garages; it's also one of the best places to come during the yearly Vegetarian Festival (p73). (ตลาดน้อย; Soi Wanit 2; ⏰7am-7pm; 🚤Tha Marine Department)

Hualamphong Train Station
HISTORIC BUILDING

7 Map p66, E3

At the southeastern edge of Chinatown, Hualamphong Train Station, Bangkok's main train terminal, was built by Dutch architects and engineers between 1910 and 1916. If you can zone out of the chaos for a moment, look for the vaulted iron roof and neoclassical portico that were a state-of-the-art engineering feat.
(สถานีรถไฟหัวลำโพง; off Th Phra Ram IV; Ⓜ Hua Lamphong exit 2)

Sampeng Lane
MARKET

8 Map p66, C2

Sampeng Lane (officially known as Soi Wanit 1) is a narrow, atmospheric artery that runs parallel to Th Yaowarat and bisects the commercial areas of Chinatown and Phahurat. The strip is bordered by tons of wholesale shops selling 'Made in China' hair accessories, pens, stickers, household goods and beeping, flashing knick-knacks, making it more interesting for the experience than the wares.
(สำเพ็ง; Soi Wanit 1; ⏰ 8am-6pm; 🚤 Tha Ratchawong, Ⓜ Hua Lamphong exit 1 & taxi)

Church of Santa Cruz
CHURCH

9 Map p66, A3

Centuries before Sukhumvit became Bangkok's international district, the Portuguese claimed *fa·ràng* (Western) supremacy, and in Thornburi built the Church of Santa Cruz in the 1700s.

The surviving church dates to 1913. Small village streets break off from the main courtyard into the area; on Soi Kuti Jiin 3, houses sell Portuguese-inspired cakes and sweets.
(โบสถ์ซังตาครูส; Soi Kuti Jiin; admission free; ⏰ 7am-noon Sat & Sun; 🚤 river-crossing ferry from Tha Pak Talat/Atsadang)

Saphan Phut Night Bazaar
MARKET

10 Map p66, B3

On the Bangkok side of Saphan Phut (also known as Memorial Bridge), this low-key night market has bucketloads of cheap clothes, late-night snacking and a lot of people-watching.
(ตลาดนัดสะพานพุทธ; Th Saphan Phut; ⏰ 8pm-midnight Tue-Sun; 🚤 Tha Saphan Phut/Memorial Bridge)

☑️ Top Tip

Bangkok Street Semantics

▶ The Thai word *tà·nǒn* (usually spelt 'thanon') means road, street or avenue. Hence Yaowarat Rd is always called Thanon (Th) Yaowarat in Thai.

▶ A soi is a small street or lane that runs off a larger street. For example, the address 48 Soi 6, Th Yaowarat will be located off Th Yaowarat on Soi 6. Alternative ways of writing the same address include 48 Th Yaowarat Soi 6, or even just 48 Soi Yaowarat 6.

NALINE CHANG / GETTY IMAGES ©

Gurdwara Siri Guru Singh Sabha

Gurdwara Siri Guru Singh Sabha

TEMPLE

11 ⊙ Map p66, B2

Just off Th Chakrawat is this gold-domed Sikh temple, allegedly one of the largest outside India. *Prasada* (blessed food offered to Hindu or Sikh temple attendees) is distributed among devotees every morning around 9am, and if you arrive on a Sikh festival day, you can partake in the *langar* (communal Sikh meal) served in the temple.

(พระศาสนสถานคุรุดวารา; off Th Chakraphet; admission free; ⊙9am-5pm; 🚤Tha Saphan Phut/Memorial Bridge)

Corrections Museum

MUSEUM

12 ⊙ Map p66, C1

Learn about the painful world of Thai-style punishment at what's left of this former jail. Life-sized models re-enact a variety of horrendous executions and punishments, encouraging most visitors to remain law-abiding citizens for the remainder of their stay.

(พิพิธภัณฑ์ราชทัณฑ์; 436 Th Mahachai; admission free; ⊙9am-4pm Mon-Fri; 🚤klorng boat to Phanfa Leelard Pier)

Understand
The Chinese Influence

In many ways Bangkok is a Chinese, as much as a Thai, city. The Chinese presence in Bangkok pre-dates the founding of the city, when Thonburi Si Mahasamut was little more than a Chinese trading outpost on Mae Nam Chao Phraya. In the 1780s, during the construction of the new capital under Rama I (King Phraphutthayotfa; r 1782–1809), Hokkien, Teochew and Hakka Chinese were hired as labourers. Eventually these labourers and entrepreneurs were relocated to the districts of Yaowarat and Sampeng, today known as Bangkok's Chinatown.

Roots in Business
During the reign of Rama I, many Chinese began to move up in status and wealth. They controlled many of Bangkok's shops and businesses, and because of increased trading ties with China, were responsible for an immense expansion in Thailand's market economy. Visiting Europeans during the 1820s were astonished by the number of Chinese trading ships on Mae Nam Chao Phraya, and some assumed that the Chinese formed the majority of Bangkok's population.

An Emerging Aristocracy
The newfound wealth of certain Chinese trading families created one of Thailand's first elite classes that was not directly related to royalty. Known as *jôw sŏo·a*, these 'merchant lords' eventually obtained additional status by accepting official posts and royal titles, as well as by offering their daughters to the royal family. At one point, Rama V (King Chulalongkorn; r 1868–1910) took a Chinese consort. Today it is believed that more than half of the people in Bangkok can claim some Chinese ancestry.

Cultural Integration
During the reign of Rama III (King Phranangklao; r 1824–51), the Thai capital began to absorb many elements of Chinese food, design, fashion and literature. By the beginning of the 20th century, the ubiquity of Chinese culture, coupled with the tendency of the Chinese men to marry Thai women and assimilate into Thai culture, had resulted in relatively little difference between the Chinese and their Siamese counterparts.

Eating

Samsara
JAPANESE, THAI $$

13 Map p66, D4

Combining Japanese and Thai dishes, Belgian beers and a retro/artsy atmosphere, Samsara is easily Chinatown's most eclectic place to eat. It's also very tasty, and the generous riverside breezes and views add to the package. The restaurant is near the end of tiny Soi Khang Wat Pathum Khongkha, just west of the temple of the same name.

(Soi Khang Wat Pathum Khongkha; mains 110-320B; ⏰4pm-midnight Tue-Thu, to 1am Fri-Sun; �; ⚓Tha Ratchawong, Ⓜ Hua Lamphong exit 1 & taxi)

Old Siam Plaza
THAI SWEETS $

14 Map p66, B1

Sugar junkies, be sure to include this stop on your Bangkok eating itinerary. The ground floor of this shopping centre is a candy land of traditional Thai sweets and snacks, most made right before your eyes.

☑ Top Tip
Day Off
Most of Bangkok's street-food vendors close up shop on Monday, so don't plan on eating in Chinatown – where much of the food is street-based – on this day.

(cnr Th Phahurat & Th Triphet; mains 30-90B; ⏰6am-7pm; ⚓Tha Saphan Phut/Memorial Bridge)

Khun Yah Cuisine
CENTRAL THAI $

15 Map p66, E3

Strategically located for a lunch break after visiting Wat Traimit, Khun Yah specialises in the full-flavoured curries, dips and stir-fries of central Thailand. But be sure to get there early; come noon many dishes are already sold out. Khun Yah Cuisine has no roman-script sign but is located just east of the Golden Buddha, in the same compound.

(off Th Mitthaphap/Traimit; mains from 40B; ⏰6am-1.30pm Mon-Fri; ⚓Tha Ratchawong, Ⓜ Hua Lamphong exit 1)

Nay Hong
THAI-CHINESE $

16 Map p66, D1

The reward for locating this hole-in-the-wall is one of the best fried noodle dishes in Bangkok. Nay Hong does gŏo·ay đĕe·o kôo·a gài, flat rice noodles fried with garlic oil, chicken and egg. To find it, from the corner of Th Sua Pa and Th Luang, proceed north, then turn right into the first side street; Nay Hong is at the end of this tiny alleyway.

(off Th Yukol 2; mains 35-50B; ⏰4-10pm; ⚓Tha Ratchawong, Ⓜ Hua Lamphong exit 1 & taxi)

Royal India

INDIAN $$

17 Map p66, B2

A windowless dining room of 10 tables in a dark alley may not be everybody's ideal lunch destination, but this legendary north Indian place continues to draw foodies despite the lack of aesthetics. Try any of the delicious breads or rich curries, and finish with a homemade Punjabi sweet.

(392/1 Th Chakraphet; mains 70-350B; ⏱10am-10pm; 🚶; 🚤Tha Saphan Phut/Memorial Bridge)

Hoon Kuang

CHINESE-THAI $

18 Map p66, D3

Serving the food of Chinatown's streets in air-con comfort is this low-key, long-standing staple. The must-eat dishes are pictured on the door, but it'd be a pity to miss the 'prawn curry flat rice noodle', a unique mash-up of two Thai-Chinese dishes – crab in curry powder and flash-fried noodles – that will make you wonder why they were ever served separately.

(381 Th Yaowarat; mains 100-200B; ⏱11am-7.45pm Mon-Sat; 🚤Tha Ratchawong, Ⓜ Hua Lamphong exit 1 & taxi)

Hua Seng Hong

CHINESE $$

19 Map p66, D2

Asian tourists come here for the shark-fin soup (which we don't recommend), but Hua Seng Hong's varied menu, which includes dim sum, braised goose feet and noodles, makes

Local Life

Waving the Yellow Flag

During the annual **Vegetarian Festival** in September/October, Bangkok's Chinatown becomes a virtual orgy of nonmeat cuisine. The festivities centre on Chinatown's main street, Th Yaowarat, and the Talat Noi area, but food shops and stalls all over the city post yellow flags to announce their meat-free status.

it a handy destination for anybody craving Chinese.

(371-373 Th Yaowarat; mains 50-1200B; ⏱9am-1am; 🚤Tha Ratchawong, Ⓜ Hua Lamphong exit 1 & taxi)

Drinking

River Vibe

BAR

20 Map p66, D4

Can't afford the drinks at Bangkok's upmarket rooftop bars? The river views from the top of this guesthouse will hardly feel like a compromise. We suggest getting dinner elsewhere, though. To find it, follow the signs to River View Guest House that start to appear along Soi Wanit 2.

(8th fl, River View Guest House, off Soi Wanit 2; ⏱7.30-10.30pm; 🚤Tha Marine Department, Ⓜ Hua Lamphong exit 1 & taxi)

Understand
The King

If you see a yellow Rolls-Royce flashing by along Bangkok avenues, accompanied by a police escort, you've probably just caught a glimpse of Thailand's longest-reigning monarch – and the longest-reigning living monarch in the world – King Bhumibol Adulyadej.

The Man on the Throne

Also known in English as Rama IX, Bhumibol Adulyadej was born in 1927 in the USA, where his father, Prince Mahidol, was studying medicine at Harvard. Fluent in English, French, German and Thai, Bhumibol ascended the throne in 1946 following the death of his brother Rama VIII (King Ananda Mahidol; r 1935–46), who reigned for just over 11 years before dying under mysterious circumstances. An ardent jazz composer and saxophonist when he was younger, Rama IX has hosted jam sessions with the likes of jazz greats Woody Herman and Benny Goodman. His compositions are often played on Thai radio. The king is also recognised for his extensive development projects, particularly in rural areas of Thailand. Rama IX and Queen Sirikit have four children: Princess Ubol Ratana (b 1951), Crown Prince Maha Vajiralongkorn (b 1952), Princess Mahachakri Sirindhorn (b 1955) and Princess Chulabhorn (b 1957).

The Twilight of an Era

After more than 60 years in power, and having recently reached his 87th birthday, Rama IX is preparing for his succession. For the last few years the Crown Prince has performed most of the royal ceremonies the king would normally perform, such as presiding over the Royal Ploughing Ceremony, changing the attire on the Emerald Buddha and handing out academic degrees at university commencements.

Royal Etiquette

Along with nation and religion, the monarchy is highly regarded in Thai society, and negative comments about Rama IX or any member of the royal family is a social, and legal, taboo. For an objective, English-language biography of the king's life and accomplishments, *King Bhumibol Adulyadej: A Life's Work* (Editions Didier Millet, 2010) is available in many Bangkok bookshops.

El Chiringuito

BAR

21 Map p66, D3

This Chinatown shophouse has been converted into a retro bar-gallery. Come for sangria, Spanish gin and bar snacks, or the art exhibitions. Opening hours can be sporadic, so call or check the Facebook page before heading out. (📞08 6340 4791; www.facebook.com/elchiringuitobangkok; 221 Soi Nana; ⏱7pm-midnight Thu-Sat; 🚤Tha Ratchawong, Ⓜ Hua Lamphong exit 1)

Entertainment

Sala Chalermkrung

THEATRE

22 ⭐ Map p66, B1

This art deco Bangkok landmark, a former cinema dating to 1933, is one of the few remaining places *kŏhn* can be witnessed. The traditional Thai dance-drama is enhanced here by laser graphics, high-tech audio and English subtitles. Concerts and other events are also held; check the website for details. (📞0 2222 0434; www.salachalermkrung.com; 66 Th Charoen Krung; tickets 800-1200B; ⏱shows 7.30pm Thu & Fri; 🚤Tha Saphan Phut/Memorial Bridge, Ⓜ Hua Lamphong exit 1 & taxi)

Top Tip

Dry Zone

Other than El Chiringuito, River Vibe and SoulBar, there's virtually zilch in the realm of non-dodgy nightlife in Bangkok's Chinatown. So fuel up on street eats here first, then head to nearby Banglamphu or Silom for drinks.

SoulBar

LIVE MUSIC

23 ⭐ Map p66, E4

An unlikely venue – and neighbourhood – for live music, this recently converted shophouse nonetheless plays host to live blues, jazz and soul from 10pm Wednesdays to Saturdays. Come earlier in the day and have coffee in a 'hood that's on the cusp of gentrification. (www.facebook.com/livesoulbarbangkok; 945 Th Charoen Krung; ⏱8.30am-12.30am; Ⓜ Hua Lamphong exit 1 & taxi)

Explore

Siam Square, Pratunam & Ploenchit

Multistorey malls, department stores, open-air shopping precincts and seemingly never-ending markets leave no doubt that Siam Square, Pratunam and Ploenchit combine to form Bangkok's commercial district. The BTS (Skytrain) interchange at Siam has also made this area the de facto centre of today's Bangkok, so you'll probably find yourself here for touristing and dining as well as shopping.

OLIVER STREWE / GETTY IMAGES ©

The Sights in a Day

☀️ Spend the morning taking in the architecture and antiques at **Jim Thompson House** (p78). If contemporary art is more your thing, check out the latest exhibition at the nearby **Bangkok Art & Culture Centre** (p82).

☀️ Cross over to the seven storeys of commerce that is **MBK Center** (p91), capping off your shopping spree with lunch at the cheap-but-tasty **MBK Food Island** (p86).

🌙 Follow the elevated Sky Walk to the **Erawan Shrine** (p82), stopping along the way at **Siam Paragon** (p92), **Siam Center** (p91) and **Central-World** (p92). Consider a spa treatment at **Thann Sanctuary** (p84) or **Spa 1930** (p82), or a cocktail treatment at **Hyde & Seek** (p89). Contrast your food-court lunch with a French feast at **Le Beaulieu** (p84) or a nouveau-Thai dinner at **Sra Bua** (p86). If you've still got it in you, get boozy with the locals at **Co-Co Walk** (p90).

👁 Top Sights
Jim Thompson House (p78)

💜 Best of Bangkok

Malls
MBK Center (p91)

Siam Center (p91)

Spas
Spa 1930 (p82)

Thann Sanctuary (p84)

Fine Dining
Sra Bua (p86)

Four Seasons Sunday Brunch (p87)

Ethnic Cuisine
Le Beaulieu (p84)

Din Tai Fung (p86)

For Kids
KidZania (p83)

Siam Ocean World (p84)

Getting There

⑤ BTS Siam, National Stadium, Chit Lom, Phloen Chit, Ratchadamri.

⚓ Klorng boat Sapan Hua Chang Pier, Pratunam Pier, Chitlom Pier, Wireless Pier.

Top Sights
Jim Thompson House

In 1959, 12 years after he single-handedly turned Thai silk into a hugely successful export business, American Jim Thompson bought a piece of land and built himself a house. It wasn't, however, any old house. Thompson's love of all things Thai saw him buy six traditional wooden homes and reconstruct them in his garden. Although Jim met a mysterious end in 1967 (p82), today Thompson's house remains, both as a museum to these unique structures and as a tribute to the man.

◉ Map p80, A2

www.jimthompsonhouse.com

Soi Kasem San 2

adult/child 100/50B

⌚9am-6pm, compulsory tours every 20min

⛴klorng boat to Sapan Hua Chang Pier,
Ⓢ National Stadium exit 1

Don't Miss

The House

Thompson adapted the six Thai structures to create a larger home in which each room had a more familiar Western function. Another departure from tradition is the way Thompson arranged each wall with its exterior side facing the house's interior. Some of the homes were brought from the old royal capital of Ayuthaya; others were pulled down and floated across the canal.

Thompson's Art Collection

Thompson's small but splendid Asian art collection is also on display in the main house; pieces include rare Chinese porcelain and Burmese, Cambodian and Thai artefacts. Thompson had a particularly astute eye for somewhat less flashy but nonetheless charming objects, such as the 19th-century mouse maze that resembles a house.

The Grounds

After the tour, be sure to poke around the house's junglelike gardens, which include a couple more structures that can be visited and ponds filled with colourful fish. The greater compound is also home to a cafe/restaurant and a shop flogging Jim Thompson–branded silk goods.

Jim Thompson Art Center

The compound also includes the **Jim Thompson Art Center** (admission free; ☉9am-5pm), a museum with revolving displays spanning a variety of media; recent exhibitions have seen contributions from the likes of Palme d'Or–winning Thai film-maker, Apichatpong Weerasethakul.

☑ Top Tips

▶ Beware of well-dressed touts in soi near Jim Thompson House who will tell you it is closed and then try to haul you off on a dodgy buying spree.

▶ The house can only be viewed via a guided tour, which is available in Chinese, English, French, Japanese and Thai.

▶ Photography is not allowed inside any of the buildings.

✕ Take a Break

On-site is the **Thompson Bar & Restaurant** (mains 160-480B; ☉noon-5pm & 6-11pm; ❄ ✎ 🗐), a convenient stop for a cold drink overlooking the garden or a Thai meal in air-con comfort. Otherwise, from Jim Thompson House it's just a short walk to MBK Food Island (p86), probably Bangkok's best food court.

A **B** **C** **D**

1

27 S Ratchathewi

23

Th Phetchaburi Tat Mai

37

Baan Krua 6

Soi 12

Th Phayathai

Soi 18

Jim Thompson House

Sapan Hua Chang Pier

Khlong Saen Saeb

2

Soi Kasem San 2

Soi Kasem San 1

Bangkok Art & Culture Centre

2

Sra Pathum Palace

33

16

12

30

KidZania

38

Siam

Siam Ocean World

National Stadium

National Stadium Sporting Precinct

29

Soi 3

Soi 2

19

Soi 1

25

Soi 10

31

Soi 4

Siam

5

Th Phra Ram I

18

20

Soi 6

21

SIAM SQUARE

Soi 7

Soi Chulalongkorn 64

3

Th Chulalongkorn

Th Phayathai

4

Th Henri Dunant

Royal Bangkok Sports Club

PATHUMWAN

5

For reviews see	
⊙ Top Sights	p78
⊙ Sights	p82
⊗ Eating	p84
⊙ Drinking	p89
⊛ Entertainment	p91
⊡ Shopping	p91

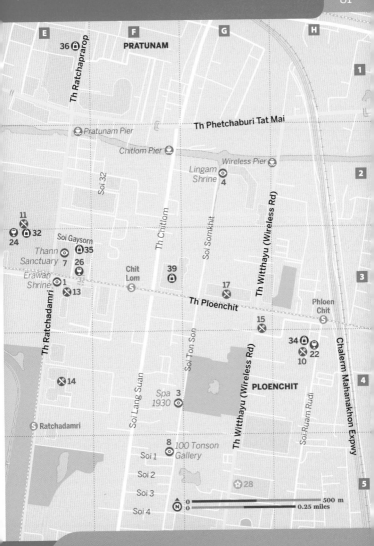

E F G H

36 🔒

PRATUNAM

Th Ratchaprarop

1

Th Phetchaburi Tat Mai

🚉 Pratunam Pier

Chitlom Pier 🚉

Wireless Pier 🚉

Lingam
Shrine 🎯
4

Soi 32

Th Chitlom

Soi Somkhit

Th Witthayu (Wireless Rd)

2

11 ❌

24 🔒 32

Soi Gaysorn

🔒 35

Thann 🎯
Sanctuary 7

26 🎯

Chit
Lom 🚉

39
🔒

17 ❌

3

Erawan
Shrine 🎯 1

❌ 13

Th Ploenchit

15 ❌

Phloen
Chit 🚉

34 🔒 🎯
22

❌
10

Chalerm Mahanakhon Expwy

Th Ratchadamri

❌ 14

Soi Lang Suan

Soi Ton Son

Spa
1930 🎯 3

PLOENCHIT

Th Witthayu (Wireless Rd)

Soi Ruam Rudi

4

🚉 Ratchadamri

8 🎯
100 Tonson
Gallery

Soi 1

Soi 2

Soi 3

Soi 4

🎯 28

Ⓝ 0   500 m
0   0.25 miles

5

Sights

Erawan Shrine

MONUMENT

1 Map p80, E3

In Bangkok, commerce and religion are not mutually exclusive. This Brahman shrine was built after accidents delayed construction of the former Erawan Hotel (today the Grand Hyatt Erawan). News of the shrine's protective powers spread and merit makers now stream into the courtyard with their own petitions; commissioning a traditional Thai dance is a popular way of saying thanks if a wish is granted.

(ศาลพระพรหม; cnr Th Ratchadamri & Th Ploenchit; admission free; ⏰6am-11pm; Ⓢ Chit Lom exit 8)

Bangkok Art & Culture Centre

ART GALLERY

2 Map p80, B2

In addition to three floors and 3000 sq metres of gallery space, this large, modern complex in the centre of Bangkok also contains arty shops, private galleries and cafes. Check the website to see what's on when you're in town.

(BACC; www.bacc.or.th; cnr Th Phayathai & Th Phra Ram I; admission free; ⏰10am-9pm Tue-Sat; Ⓢ National Stadium exit 3)

Spa 1930

SPA

3 Map p80, F4

Discreet and sophisticated, Spa 1930 rescues relaxers from the contrived spa ambience of New Age music and

---

Understand
Jim Thompson

Born in Delaware in 1906, Jim Thompson served in a forerunner of the CIA in Thailand during WWII. When, in 1947, he spotted some silk in a market and was told it was woven in Baan Krua, he found the only place in Bangkok where silk was still woven by hand. Thompson's Thai silk eventually attracted the interest of fashion houses in New York, Milan, London and Paris, and he gradually built a worldwide clientele for a craft that had been in danger of dying out.

In March 1967 Thompson went missing while out for an afternoon walk in the Cameron Highlands of western Malaysia. Thompson has never been heard from since, but the conspiracy theories have never stopped. Was it communist spies? Business rivals? A man-eating tiger? Although the mystery has never been solved, evidence revealed by journalist Joshua Kurlantzick in his profile of Thompson, *The Ideal Man*, suggests that the vocal anti-American stance Thompson took later in his life may have made him a potential target of suppression by the CIA.

Erawan Shrine

ingredients you'd rather see at a dinner party. The menu is simple (face, body care and body massage) and the scrubs and massage oils are logical players.
(📞0 2254 8606; www.spa1930.com; 42 Soi Ton Son; Thai massage from 1200B, spa packages from 3800B; ⏰9.30am-9.30pm; 🚇Chit Lom exit 4)

Lingam Shrine

MONUMENT

4 ◉ Map p80, G2

This little shrine that is situated at the back of Swissôtel Nai Lert Park was built for the spirit of a nearby tree. But soon word spread that the shrine had fertility powers and a small forest of wooden phalluses sprung up, resulting in one of Bangkok's bawdiest shrines.
(ศาลเจ้าแม่ทับทิม; Swissôtel Nai Lert Park, Th Witthayu/Wireless Rd; admission free; ⏰24hr; 🚤klorng boat to Wireless Pier, 🚇Phloen Chit exit 1)

KidZania

PLAY CENTRE

5 ◉ Map p80, C2

Your children can fly a plane, record an album, make sushi or, er, perform a root canal at this new and impressive learn-and-play centre.
(📞0 2683 1888; bangkok.kidzania.com; 5th fl, Siam Paragon, 991/1 Th Phra Ram I; adult/child 480/850B; ⏰10am-5pm Sun-Fri, 10am-3pm & 4-9pm Sat; 🚇Siam exits 3 & 5)

Baan Krua
NEIGHBOURHOOD

6 Map p80, A1

Baan Krua dates back to the turbulent years at the end of the 18th century, when Muslims from Cambodia and Vietnam fought on the side of the new Thai king and were rewarded with this plot of land. The immigrants brought their silk-weaving traditions with them, and the community grew when the residents built the adjacent canal to better connect themselves to the river. (บ้านครัว; klorng boat to Sapan Hua Chang Pier, S National Stadium exit 1)

Thann Sanctuary
SPA

7 Map p80, E3

This local brand of herbal-based soaps, lotions and cosmetics has launched a chain of mall-based spas – the perfect solution for post-shopping therapy. Also in CentralWorld (p92). (0 2658 0550; www.thann.info; 4th fl, Gaysorn Plaza, cnr Th Ploenchit & Th Ratchadamri;

Top Tip

Making Sense of Bangkok Street Names

Bangkok street names often seem unpronounceable; the inconsistency of romanised Thai spellings doesn't help. For example, the street Th Ratchadamri is sometimes spelt 'Rajdamri'. And one of the most popular locations for foreign embassies is known both as Wireless Rd and Th Witthayu (wí·tá·yú is Thai for 'radio').

Thai massage from 1500B, spa treatments from 2800B; 10am-9pm; S Chit Lom exit 9)

100 Tonson Gallery
ART GALLERY

8 Map p80, F5

Housed in a spacious villa, and regarded as one of the city's top commercial galleries, 100 Tonson hosts a variety of contemporary exhibitions of all genres by local and international artists. (www.100tonsongallery.com; 100 Soi Ton Son; admission free; 11am-7pm Thu-Sun; S Chit Lom exit 4)

Siam Ocean World
AQUARIUM

9 Map p80, D3

More than 400 species of fish, crustaceans and even penguins populate this vast underground facility. Diving with sharks (for a fee) is also an option if you have your diving licence, though you'll have almost as much fun timing your trip to coincide with the shark and penguin feedings; the former are usually at 1pm and 4pm, the latter at 12.30pm and 4.30pm – check the website for details. (สยามโอเชี่ยนเวิร์ล; www.siamoceanworld. com; basement, Siam Paragon, 991/1 Th Phra Ram I; adult/child from 713/563B; 10am-9pm; S Siam exits 3 & 5)

Eating

Le Beaulieu
FRENCH $$$

10 Map p80, H4

This is classic French dining, with the occasional and subtle local twist.

Understand

The Food of Bangkok
- -

Geography, the influence of the royal palace and the Chinese and Muslim minorities have all pitched in to shape the local cuisine.

Central Thai Cuisine

The people of central Thailand are fond of sweet/savoury flavours, and many dishes include freshwater fish, pork, coconut milk and palm sugar. Central Thai eateries, particularly those in Bangkok, also serve a wide variety of seafood. Classic central Thai dishes include *yam blah dùk foo* (fried shredded catfish, chilli and peanuts served with a sweet/tart mango dressing) and *gaang sôm* (seafood, vegetables and/or herbs in a thick, tart broth).

Royal Thai Cuisine

A key influence on the city's kitchens has been the Bangkok-based royal court, which has been producing refined takes on central Thai dishes for nearly 300 years. Although previously available only within the palace walls, these so-called 'royal' Thai dishes can now be found across the city. One enduring example of royal cuisine is *mèe gròrp*, crispy noodles made the traditional way with a sweet/sour dressing.

Chinese-Thai Cuisine

Immigrants from southern China probably introduced the wok and several varieties of noodle dishes to Thailand. They also influenced Bangkok's cuisine in other ways: beef is not widely eaten in Bangkok due to a Chinese-Buddhist teaching that forbids eating 'large' animals. Perhaps the most common example of Thai-Chinese food is *kôw man gài*, Hainanese-style chicken rice.

Muslim-Thai Cuisine

Muslims are thought to have first visited Thailand during the late 14th century. They brought with them a cuisine based on meat and dried spices. Some Muslim dishes, such as *roh·đee*, a fried bread similar to the Indian *paratha*, have changed little, if at all. Others, such as *gaang mát·sà·màn*, a rich curry, are a unique blend of Thai and Indian/Middle Eastern cooking styles and ingredients.

Yet where most places would aim for mild and beautiful, Le Beaulieu sets its sights for flavour. The tall dining room, with its equally imposing art, manages to feel both modern and classic. If dinner is out of the question budget-wise, stop by for lunch, when three-course sets are 695B and 995B.

Local Life
Dining on the Cheap

The mall-based food courts in this part of town are cheap, clean, boast English-language menus and are increasingly stylish and inviting. Our faves:

MBK Food Island (Map p80, B3; 6th fl, MBK Center, cnr Th Phra Ram I & Th Phayathai; mains 35-150B; ⊙10am-10pm; ❄ 🚼 📖; S National Stadium exit 4) The biggest and best.

Eatthai (Map p80, G3; www.facebook.com/EatthaibyCentral?rf=1493909810820988; basement, Central Embassy, 1031 Th Ploenchit; mains 60-360B; ⊙10am-10pm; ❄ 🚼 📖; S Phloen Chit exit 5) Here you'll find branches of several 'famous' stalls and restaurants.

Food Republic (Map p80, C2; 4th fl, Siam Center, cnr Th Phra Ram I & Th Phayathai; mains 30-200B; ⊙10am-10pm; ❄ 🚼 📖; S Siam exit 1) Probably Bangkok's most attractive food court.

FoodPark (Map p80, E2; 4th fl, Big C, 97/11 Th Ratchadamri; mains 30-90B; ⊙9am-9pm; ❄ 📖; S Chit Lom exit 9 to Sky Walk) A Thai food court for Thais.

(🕿02 168 8220; ground fl, Athenee Office Tower, 63 Th Witthayu/Wireless Rd ; mains 1450-2450B; ⊙11.30am-2.30pm & 6.30-11.30pm Tue-Sun; ❄ 📖; S Phloen Chit exits 2 & 4)

Din Tai Fung
CHINESE $$

11 Map p80, E2

Most come to this lauded Taiwanese franchise for the *xiao long bao*, broth-filled 'soup' dumplings. And so should you. But the northern Chinese–style fare is generally tasty, and justifies exploring the more distant regions of the menu.

(7th fl, CentralWorld, Th Ratchadamri; ⊙11am-10pm; ❄ 🚼 📖; S Chit Lom exit 9 to Sky Walk, Siam exit 6 to Sky Walk)

Sra Bua
THAI $$$

12 Map p80, D2

Helmed by a Thai and a Dane whose Copenhagen restaurant, Kiin Kiin, snagged a Michelin star, Sra Bua takes a correspondingly international approach to Thai food. Putting local ingredients through the wringer of molecular gastronomy, the couple have created unconventional Thai dishes such as 'frozen red curry with lobster salad'. Reservations are recommended.

(🕿0 2162 9000; www.kempinskibangkok.com/sra-bua-by-kiin-kiin; ground fl, Siam Kempinski Hotel, 991/9 off Th Phra Ram I; set meals 2700B; ⊙noon-3pm & 6-11pm; ❄ 📖; S Siam exits 3 & 5)

MBK Food Island

Crystal Jade La Mian Xiao Long Bao

CHINESE $$

13 Map p80, E3

The tongue-twistingly long name of this Singaporean chain refers to the restaurant's signature *la mian* (wheat noodles) and the famous Shanghainese *xiao long bao* ('soup' dumplings). If you order the hand-pulled noodles (which you should do), allow the staff to cut them with kitchen shears, otherwise you'll end up with ample evidence of your meal on your shirt. (basement, Erawan Bangkok, 494 Th Ploenchit; mains 110-1050B; ⊙11am-10pm; ✳✎⊡; Ⓢ Chit Lom exit 8)

Four Seasons Sunday Brunch

INTERNATIONAL $$$

14 Map p80, E4

All of the Four Seasons' highly regarded restaurants – Spice Market, Shintaro, Biscotti and Madison – set up steam tables in the same room for this decadent Sunday brunch buffet. Numerous cooking stations and champagne options take this light years beyond the standard Sunday brunch. It's obtained institutional status, so be sure to reserve your table a couple of weeks in advance. (☎0 2126 8866, ext 1231; www.fourseasons.com/bangkok/dining/restaurants/sunday_brunch; ground fl, Four Seasons Hotel, 155 Th Ratchadamri; buffet 3473B; ⊙11.30am-3pm Sun; ✳✎⊡; Ⓢ Ratchadamri exit 4)

Sanguan Sri
CENTRAL THAI **$**

15 Map p80, G3

This restaurant, essentially a concrete bunker filled with furniture circa 1973, can afford to remain decidedly *cher-i* (old-fashioned) because of its reputation. Mimic the area's hungry office staff and try central Thai dishes such as the *gaang pèt ʾbèt yâhng* (red curry with grilled duck breast served over snowy white rice noodles). No roman-script sign.

(59/1 Th Witthayu/Wireless Rd; mains 40-150B; ⏰10am-3pm Mon-Sat; ✳️📶; **S** Phloen Chit exit 5)

Nuer Koo
CHINESE-THAI **$**

16 Map p80, C2

Is this the future of the noodle stall? Mall-bound Nuer Koo does an indoor version of the formerly humble bowl of beef noodles. Choose your cut of beef – including Kobe beef from Japan – enjoy the rich broth and cool air-con, and quickly forget about the good old days.

(4th fl, Siam Paragon, 991/1 Th Phra Ram I; mains 85-970B; ⏰11.30am-10pm; ✳️📶; **S** Siam exits 3 & 5)

Water Library
FRENCH, INTERNATIONAL **$$$**

17 Map p80, G3

The Eiffel Tower–themed dining room of this successful local chain is a slightly cheesy indication of its effort toward French-influenced bistro fare. But the food is serious, taking the form of decadent twists on humble faves, such as a *croque-monsieur* stuffed with prosciutto instead of ham.

(📞0 2160 5893; www.waterlibrary.com; 5th fl, Central Embassy, 1031 Th Ploenchit; mains 350-1150B; ⏰10am-10pm Sun-Thu, to midnight Fri-Sat; ✳️📶; **S** Phloen Chit exit 5)

Som Tam Nua
NORTHEASTERN THAI **$**

18 Map p80, C3

It can't compete with the street stalls for flavour or authenticity, but if you need to be seen, particularly in trendy, air-con surroundings, this is a good place to sample northeastern Thai specialities. Expect a lengthy queue at dinner.

(392/14 Soi 5, Siam Sq; mains 75-120B; ⏰10.45am-9.30pm; ✳️📶; **S** Siam exit 4)

Koko
THAI **$**

19 Map p80, C3

Perfect for both omnivores and vegetarians, this casual cafelike restaurant offers a lengthy veggie menu, not to mention a brief but solid repertoire of meat-based Thai dishes, such as a Penang curry served with tender pork, or fish deep-fried and served with Thai herbs.

(262/2 Soi 3, Siam Sq; mains 75-240B; ⏰11am-9pm; ✳️🖊️📶; **S** Siam exit 2)

Food Plus
THAI **$**

20 Map p80, C3

This claustrophobic alleyway is bursting with the wares of several *râhn kôw gaang* (rice and curry stalls). Most dishes are made ahead of time, so simply point to what looks tasty.

AUSTIN BUSH / GETTY IMAGES ©

Siam Paragon (p92)

You'll be hard-pressed to spend more than 100B, and the flavours are unanimously authentic.

(btwn Soi 5 & Soi 6, Siam Sq; mains 30-70B; ⏰9am-3pm; 📱; **S**Siam exit 2)

Coca Suki   CHINESE, THAI $$

21 Map p80, D3

Immensely popular with Thai families, *sù·gêe* takes the form of a bubbling hotpot of broth and the raw ingredients to dip therein. Coca is one of the oldest purveyors of the dish, and this branch reflects the brand's efforts to appear more modern. Fans of spice, be sure to request the tangy 'tom yam' broth.

(416/3-8 Th Henri Dunant; mains 98-688B; ⏰11am-11pm; ❄ 🍴 📱; **S**Siam exit 6)

Drinking
Hyde & Seek   BAR

22 🍷 Map p80, H4

The tasty and comforting English-inspired snacks and meals here have earned Hyde & Seek bar the right to call itself a 'gastrobar'. But we reckon the real reasons to come here are what is arguably Bangkok's best-stocked liquor cabinet, and some of the city's tastiest and most sophisticated cocktails.

(www.hydeandseek.com; ground fl, Athenee Residence, 65/1 Soi Ruam Rudi; ⏰11am-1am; **S**Phloen Chit exit 4)

Co-Co Walk

BAR

23 Map p80, B1

This covered compound is a smorgasbord of pubs, bars and live music, and is popular with Thai university students. It's a fun, low-key place to drink like the locals do.

(87/70 Th Phayathai; ⏰5pm-midnight; ⑤Ratchathewi exit 2)

Red Sky

BAR

24 Map p80, E3

Perched on the 55th floor of a sleek skyscraper, Bangkok's newest rooftop venture feels a bit more formal than most and, as such, boasts an extensive wine list and a Martini menu. As is the case with most of Bangkok's rooftop bars, those wearing shorts and/or sandals aren't welcome to the party.

(www.centarahotelsresorts.com/redsky; 55th fl, Centara Grand, CentralWorld, Th Ratchadamri; ⏰6pm-1am; ⑤Chit Lom exit 9 to Sky Walk, Siam exit 6 to Sky Walk)

To-Sit

BAR

25 Map p80, C3

Live, loud and sappy music; cheap and spicy food; good friends and cold beer: To-Sit epitomises everything a Thai university student could wish for on a night out. There are branches all over town (check the website), but the Siam Sq location has the advantage of being virtually the only option in an area that's buzzing during the day but dead at night.

(www.tosit.com; Soi 3, Siam Sq; ⑤Siam exit 2)

Mixx

CLUB

26 Map p80, E3

As the name suggests, Mixx draws a wide swathe of Bangkok's partiers, from backpackers to working girls, making it the least dodgy of Bangkok's late-night discos.

(mixx-discotheque.com/bangkok; basement, InterContinental Hotel, 973 Th Ploenchit; admission 300B; ⏰10pm-2am; ⑤Chit Lom exit 7)

Ⓠ Local Life

Siam Square's Silver Screens

The Siam Sq area is home to Bangkok's ritziest cinemas. Each mall has its own theatre, but **Paragon Cineplex** (Map p80, C2; 📞0 2129 4635; www.paragoncineplex.com; 5th fl, Siam Paragon, 991/1 Th Phra Ram I; ⑤Siam exits 3 & 5), with its IMAX screen (Thailand's largest) and semiprivate luxury cinemas, comes out on top. For something less flashy, consider the old-school stand-alone theatres just across the street: **Scala** (Map p80, B3; 📞0 2251 2861; Soi 1, Siam Sq; ⑤Siam exit 2) and **Lido** (Map p80, C3; 📞0 2252 6498; www.apexsiam-square.com; btwn Soi 2 & Soi 3, Siam Sq; ⑤Siam exit 2).

Entertainment

Playhouse Theater Cabaret

CABARET

27 ⭐ Map p80, B1

Watching *gà·teu·i* (ladyboys; also spelt *kàthoey*) perform show tunes has become the latest 'must-do' fixture on the Bangkok tourist circuit. Playhouse caters to the trend with choreographed stage shows featuring Broadway high kicks and lip-synched pop tunes. (📞0 2215 0571; www.playhousethailand. com; basement, Asia Hotel, 296 Th Phayathai; admission 1200B; ⏱show times 8.15pm & 9.45pm; **S** Ratchathewi exit 1)

Diplomat Bar

LIVE MUSIC

28 ⭐ Map p80, G5

Named for its location in the middle of the embassy district, this is one of the few hotel lounges that locals make a point of visiting. Choose from an expansive list of innovative Martinis and sip along to live jazz, gracefully played at conversation level. (ground fl, Conrad Hotel, 87 Th Witthayu/Wireless Rd; ⏱7pm-1am Sun-Thu, to 2am Fri & Sat; **S** Phloen Chit exit 5)

Shopping

MBK Center

SHOPPING CENTRE

29 🔒 Map p80, B3

This immense shopping mall has become one of Bangkok's top attractions. Swedish and other foreign languages

Top Tip

Living Large

In your home town you may be considered average or even petite, but in Thailand you're likely an extra large, clearly marked on the tag as 'XL'. If that batters the body image, then skip the street markets, where the sizes are even smaller. Instead, for formal wear, many expats turn to custom tailors, while many of the vendors at Pratunam Market and several stalls on the 7th floor of MBK Center stock larger sizes.

can be heard as much as Thai, and on any given weekend half of Bangkok can be found here combing through an inexhaustible range of stalls and shops stocking mobile phones, accessories, shoes, camera equipment, handbags and T-shirts. (www.mbk-center.com; cnr Th Phra Ram I & Th Phayathai; ⏱10am-10pm; **S** National Stadium exit 4)

Siam Center

SHOPPING CENTRE

30 🔒 Map p80, C2

Siam Center, Thailand's first shopping centre, was built in 1976 but, since a recent nip and tuck, it hardly shows its age. Its 3rd floor is one of the best locations in Bangkok to check out established local labels such as **Flynow III**, **Senada Theory** and **Tango**, among others. (Th Phra Ram I; ⏱10am-9pm; **S** Siam exit 1)

Siam Square

SHOPPING CENTRE

31 🔒 Map p80, C3

Siam Square is ground zero for teenage culture in Bangkok. Pop music blares out of speakers, and gangs of teens in costumes ricochet between fast-food restaurants and closet-sized boutiques. Several shops peddle pop-hip styles along Soi 2 and Soi 3, but most outfits require a 'barely there' waist. (Th Phra Ram I; ⏰11am-9pm; S Siam exits 2, 4 & 6)

CentralWorld

SHOPPING CENTRE

32 🔒 Map p80, E3

Spanning eight storeys and more than 500 shops and 100 restaurants, CentralWorld is one of Southeast Asia's largest shopping centres. In addition to an ice rink, you'll find a huge branch of bookstore **B2S**, and fragrances at Karmakamet on the 3nd floor. (www.centralworld.co.th; Th Ratchadamri; ⏰10am-10pm; S Chit Lom exit 9 to Sky Walk, Siam exit 6 to Sky Walk)

Siam Paragon

SHOPPING CENTRE

33 🔒 Map p80, C2

Paragon, 'The Pride of Bangkok', epitomises the city's fanaticism for the new and the excessive. In addition to the usual high-end brands, there's a Lamborghini dealer on the 2nd floor, and one floor up the True Urban Park 'lifestyle centre' featuring a cafe, internet access and a shop selling books and music. (www.siamparagon.co.th; 991/1 Th Phra Ram I; ⏰10am-10pm; S Siam exits 3 & 5)

Pinky Tailors

CLOTHING

34 🔒 Map p80, H4

Suit jackets have been Mr Pinky's speciality for 35 years. His custom-made dress shirts, for both men and women,

Local Life
Local Brands Worth Buying

Forget those creaking wooden frogs and embroidered elephants: today's Bangkok has a more sophisticated range of souvenirs. Consider:

Thann (Map p80, E2; www.thann.info; 2nd fl, CentralWorld, Th Ratchadamri; ⏰10am-10pm; S Chit Lom exit 9 to Sky Walk, Siam exit 6 to Sky Walk), with great botanical-based spa products.

Karmakamet (Map p80, E2; www.karmakamet.co.th; 3rd fl, CentralWorld, Th Ratchadamri; ⏰10am-9.30pm; S Chit Lom exit 9 to Sky Walk, Siam exit 6 to Sky Walk), with an amazing range of scents.

Propaganda (Map p80, B2; 4th fl, Siam Discovery Center, cnr Th Phra Ram I & Th Phayathai; ⏰10am-9pm; S Siam exit 1), where MR P, the brand's signature character, appears in cartoon lamps and other products.

Doi Tung (Map p80, B2; www.doitung.org; 4th fl, Siam Discovery Center, cnr Th Phra Ram I & Th Phayathai; ⏰10am-9pm; S Siam exit 1) Consider the attractive hand-woven carpets and handsome ceramics here.

also have dedicated fans. Located behind the Mahatun Building.
(www.pinkytailor.com; 888/40 Mahatun Plaza, Th Ploenchit; ⊙10am-7pm Mon-Sat; **S**Phloen Chit exits 2 & 4)

Narai Phand SOUVENIRS

35 Map p80, E3

Souvenir-quality handicrafts are given fixed prices and sold in air-conditioned comfort at this government-run facility. You won't find anything here that you haven't already seen at the street markets, but it is a good stop if you're pressed for time or are spooked by haggling.
(www.naraiphand.com; ground fl, President Tower, 973 Th Ploenchit; ⊙10am-8pm; **S**Chit Lom exit 7)

Pratunam Market CLOTHING

36 Map p80, E1

The emphasis in Bangkok's de facto garment district is on cheap clothes, and you could spend hours flipping through the T-shirts at the seemingly endless **Baiyoke Garment Center**. It doesn't end there: across the street is the five-storey **Platinum Fashion Mall**, which sports the latest in no-brand couture.
(cnr Th Phetchaburi Tat Mai & Th Ratchaprarop; ⊙10am-10pm; ☸klorng boat to Pratunam Pier, **S**Ratchathewi exit 4)

Pantip Plaza SHOPPING CENTRE

37 Map p80, D1

If you can tolerate the crowds and annoying pornography vendors ('DVD sex? DVD sex?'), Pantip, a multistorey computer and electronics warehouse, might just be your kinda paradise. Technocrati will find pirated software and music, gear for hobbyists to enhance their machines, flea-market-style peripherals and other odds and ends.
(604 Th Phetchaburi Tat Mai; ⊙10am-9pm; **S**Ratchathewi exit 4)

Siam Discovery Center SHOPPING CENTRE

38 Map p80, B2

A modern mall with a few interesting domestic outlets such as Doi Tung (p92) and Propaganda (p92). Kids might be drawn to the branch of **Madame Tussaud's** on the 6th floor.
(cnr Th Phra Ram I & Th Phayathai; ⊙10am-10pm; **S**Siam exit 1)

Central Chidlom SHOPPING CENTRE

39 Map p80, F3

Central is a modern Western-style department store with locations throughout the city. This flagship shop, Thailand's largest, is the snazziest of all the branches.
(www.central.co.th; 1027 Th Ploenchit; ⊙10am-10pm; **S**Chit Lom exit 5)

Local Life
Victory Monument & Around

Getting There

S **BTS** Phaya Thai and Victory Monument

For a glimpse of Bangkok without the touts, tourists or malls (well, OK, some malls – this is, after all, Bangkok), take the BTS north to the area around the Victory Monument, where you'll find ordinary Thais doing ordinary Thai things, not to mention a handful of worthwhile attractions, good restaurants and fun bars.

❶ Suan Pakkad Palace Museum

This **former royal residence** (วังสวนผัก กาด; Th Si Ayuthaya; admission 100B; ◷9am-4pm; **S**Phaya Thai exit 4) consists of eight traditional wooden Thai houses. Within the stilt buildings are displays of art, antiques and furnishings. The landscaped grounds are a peaceful oasis in an otherwise urban area.

❷ Aksra Theatre

Get a brief fix of culture at the restaurant of this **theatre** (☎09 2205 8888, ext 5702; 3rd fl, King Power Complex, 8/1 Th Rang Nam; admission 500-800B; ◷performances 12.30-1pm & 6.30-7pm; **S**Victory Monument exit 2), where, along with a buffet Thai meal, you can catch a performance of the *Ramakian* starring knee-high puppets which need three puppeteers.

❸ Raintree

Raintree (116/63-64 Th Rang Nam; ◷6pm-1am Mon-Sat; **S**Victory Monument exit 2) is one of the few places in town to host performances of 'songs for life', Thai folk music with roots in the communist insurgency of the 1960s and '70s.

❹ Pathé

The modern Thai equivalent of a 1950s-era American diner, **Pathé** (www.patherestaurant.com; 507 Th Ratchawithi; mains 80-250B; ◷2pm-1am; **S**Victory Monument exit 4) combines solid Thai food, a fun atmosphere and a jukebox.

❺ Fashion Mall

Cheap women's underwear, domestic cosmetics and an entire zone of hair extensions – **Fashion Mall** (Th Ratchawithi; ◷10.30am-midnight; **S**Victory Monument exit 2) is the place to go to outfit yourself like a Thai university student on a budget.

❻ Victory Monument

The obelisk **Victory Monument** (อนุสาวรีย์ชัย; cnr Th Ratchawithi & Th Phayathai; ◷24hr; **S**Victory Monument exit 2) was built by the then military government in 1941 to commemorate a 1940 campaign against the French in Laos.

❼ Saxophone Pub & Restaurant

After more than 30 years, **Saxophone** (www.saxophonepub.com; 3/8 Th Phayathai; ◷7.30pm-1.30am; **S**Victory Monument exit 2) remains one of Bangkok's premier live-music venues – an intimate space where you can get up close to the band.

❽ Sky Train Jazz Club

The **Sky Train Jazz Club** (cnr Th Rang Nam & Th Phayathai; ◷5pm-2am; **S**Victory Monument exit 2) is more like the rooftop of your stoner buddy's flat than any jazz club we've ever been to. But that's what makes it so fun. To find it, look for the sign and proceed up the graffiti-covered stairway until you reach the roof.

❾ Wine Pub

If the upmarket but chilled setting and the DJ aren't reason enough to visit **Wine Pub** (www.pullmanbangkok-kingpower; 1st fl, Pullman Bangkok King Power, 8/2 Th Rang Nam; ◷6.30pm-2am; **S**Victory Monument exit 2), the fact that it's one of the cheapest places in Bangkok to drink wine and nibble imported cheeses and cold cuts should be.

Explore

Riverside, Silom & Lumphini

Although you may not see it behind the office blocks, high-rise condos and hotels, Mae Nam Chao Phraya (Chao Phraya River) forms a watery backdrop to these linked neighbourhoods. History is still palpable in the riverside area's crumbling architecture, while heading inland, Silom, Bangkok's de facto financial district, is frenetic and modern, and adjacent Lumphini Park serves as the city's green lung.

The Sights in a Day

If you're a morning person – or jet-lag has coerced you into being one – get an early start on the day at **Lumphini Park** (p102). Follow this with a visit to the quirky antivenom factory that is the **Queen Saovabha Memorial Institute** (p102).

Lunch on the famous fried chicken at **Kai Thort Jay Kee** (p106), then pop into **Sri Mariamman Temple** (p103) followed by a look at the latest photography exhibition at **Kathmandu Photo Gallery** (p102). Spend the remainder of the afternoon window-shopping for antiques at **House of Chao** (p113) and **River City** (p113).

Have a sunset cocktail at **Viva & Aviv** (p112), then board a ship for a **dinner cruise** (p108) along Mae Nam Chao Phraya. Alternatively, head inland and down a rooftop cocktail at **Moon Bar** (p109) followed by dinner at **nahm** (p105), home to some of the best Thai food in Bangkok.

For a local's evening in gay Silom, see p98.

 Local Life

Gay Silom (p98)

 Best of Bangkok

Fine Dining
nahm (p105)

Eat Me (p106)

Le Du (p108)

Rooftop Bars
Moon Bar (p109)

Sky Bar (p110)

Thai Massage
Health Land (p103)

Ruen-Nuad Massage Studio (p102)

For Kids
Lumphini Park (p102)

Queen Saovabha Memorial Institute (p102)

Getting There

Ⓢ **BTS** Sala Daeng, Ratchadamri, Chong Nonsi, Surasak and Saphan Taksin.

Ⓜ **MRT** Si Lom and Lumphini.

⛴ **River ferry** Tha Sathon/Central Pier, Tha Oriental, Tha Si Phraya, River City Pier and Tha Marine Department.

Local Life
Gay Silom

The side streets off lower Th Silom are so camp that they make San Francisco look like rural Texas. In addition to heaps of gay locals and tourists, the area is also home to a smattering of massage parlours and saunas, the in-your-face sex shows of nearby Duangthawee Plaza, the chilled open-air bars on Soi 4 and the clubs near Soi 2.

1 Telephone & Balcony

Commence your evening on Soi 4, arguably Bangkok's pinkest street. It's packed with predominantly gay shops, bars, clubs and restaurants. The best views of the action are from streetside bars **Telephone Pub** (www.telephonepub. com; 114/11-13 Soi 4, Th Silom; ⊙6pm-1am; 🛜; Ⓜ Si Lom exit 2, Ⓢ Sala Daeng exit 1) and, directly across the street, **Balcony** (www. balconypub.com; 86-88 Soi 4, Th Silom; ⊙5pm-2am; 🛜; Ⓜ Si Lom exit 2, Ⓢ Sala Daeng exit 1).

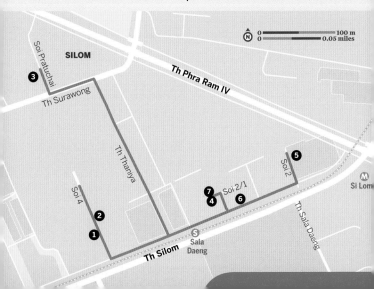

❷ Bearbie

A bear bar as perceived through the Thai lens, **Bearbie** (2nd fl, 82 Soi 4, Th Silom; ⏰8pm-1am Tue-Thu, to 2am Fri-Sun; Ⓜ️Si Lom exit 2, Ⓢ Sala Daeng exit 1) replaces beards and bikers with local 'chubs' and teddy-bear-themed karaoke rooms.

❸ Duangthawee Plaza

Finding the Soi 4 scene a tad too tame? Cross over to **Duangthawee Plaza** (Soi Twilight; Soi Pratuchai; ⏰7pm-1am; Ⓜ️Si Lom exit 2, Ⓢ Sala Daeng exit 3), a strip of male-only go-go bars (sample names: Hot Male, Banana Bar, Dream Boy) that is the gay equivalent of nearby Th Patpong. Expect tacky sex shows performed by bored-looking young men.

❹ Men Factory

If you're into the sauna scene, **Men Factory** (www.mfsauna.com; Soi 2/1, Th Silom; admission 150B; ⏰noon-2am; Ⓜ️Si Lom exit 2, Ⓢ Sala Daeng exit 1) offers the entire spectrum of options, from Thai massage on a daily basis, to nude nights on Wednesday, Friday and Sunday.

❺ DJ Station

DJ Station (www.dj-station.com; 8/6-8 Soi 2, Th Silom; admission from 150B; ⏰10pm-2am; Ⓜ️Si Lom exit 2, Ⓢ Sala Daeng exit 1) is one of Bangkok's most legendary gay dance clubs. Get there at 11.30pm for the nightly cabaret show, or later for a packed house of Thai guppies (gay professionals), prostitutes and a few Westerners. There are several similar dance clubs and bars crammed into this tiny street. Admission ranges from 150B to 300B.

❻ Silom Society

Take a breather, fuel up, or simply partake in one of the area's more low-key gay scenes at **Silom Society** (12/3 Th Silom; ⏰9am-2am; 🛜; Ⓜ️Si Lom exit 2, Ⓢ Sala Daeng exit 1), a coffee shop that stays open late.

❼ G Bangkok

Three floors barely supporting a mostly muscly/expat crowd partying to one of the area's better soundtracks, **G Bangkok** (Guys on Display; Soi 2/1, Th Silom; admission 300B; ⏰11pm-late; Ⓜ️Si Lom exit 2, Ⓢ Sala Daeng exit 1) is the place to go after DJ Station (and just about every other bar in town) has already closed. Admission 300B.

TALAT NOI

Soi 22

Tha Marine Department

River City Pier

43
36

Tha Si Phraya/ River City

17

Soi 39

Soi 41

Soi 43

Soi 32

Mae Nam Chao Phraya

Th Maha Phrutharam

Phayathai–Bangkok Expwy

Th Maha Nakhon

Soi Sawang

Saphan Tia

Sam Yan

Th Sri Phraya

Th Si Phraya

Bangkokian Museum
2

BANGRAK

Th Naret

Neilson Hays Library **13**

Th Surawong

Soi 1

24

Th Decho

Th Sap

Th Silom

41

30

9 Oriental Spa

39

Soi 36

20

Tha Oriental

49 47

Soi 40 (Soi Oriental)

48

Th Mahesak

32
Soi 32

Soi 30

Soi 28

Soi 26

46

10
Silom Galleria

18

Sri Mariamman Temple
7

Kathmandu

Photo Gallery
3

H Gallery
12

33

Soi 10

19

Soi 21

Th Surasak

34

Soi 19

Th Pramuan

25

21

Th Pan

6 Health Land
Soi 12

Soi 44

50

Soi 46

Soi Si Wiang

Soi St Louis 2

Soi St Louis 3

Saphan Taksin

Soi 50

Saphan Taksin

Th Sathon Neua (North)

Th Sathon Tai (South)

Surasak

Th Sathon Tai (South)

Tha Sathon/ Central Pier

Th Charoen Krung

Soi Pikun

Soi Pichai

Soi St Louis 2

E

F

G

H

Queen
Saovabha
Memorial **5**
Institute

Th Sarasin

Th Lang
Suan

Soi Sanam
Khlii (Soi Polo)

1

16 ✖

SILOM

Th Phra Ram IV

Th Henri Dunant

Th Ratchadamri

Lumphini
Park

1 ⊙

2

Soi
Patpong 2

44

Th Witthayu (Wireless Rd)

✖**22**

40

Soi
Patpong 1

Thanya

26

Soi 4

45 **42**

Soi 2

Ⓜ Si Lom

Th Phra Ram IV

Soi
Than
Tawan

51 **35**

Th Silom

Soi Yada

Ⓢ Sala Daeng

31

Soi Sala
Daeng 2

Th Sala Daeng

Soi Sala Daeng 1

Th Phra Ram IV

Ⓜ
Lumphini

23

Soi 5 (Soi
Lalai Sap)

Soi 3

✖**15**

Th Convent

Soi Phiphat 2

Ruen-Nuad **4**
Massage Studio

Th Sathon Tai (South)

11 ⊙ **28**
Banyan
✖ Tree Spa
14

Soi 1 (Atakanprasit)

2

Ⓢ
Chong
Nonsi

37

Th Sathon Neua (North)
Th Sathon Tai (South)

Soi 5

3

38

Soi Si
Bamphen

Soi 3

Soi 5

Soi 7 (Soi Phra Phinit)

MR Kukrit
Pramoj House
8

29

Soi Nantha

Soi Suan Phlu

4

Th Narathiwat Ratchanakharin (Chong Nonsi)

SATHON

Soi Ngam Duphli

Soi Ngam Duphli

Th Yen Akat

5

Ⓝ

0   500 m
0   0.25 miles

Sights

Lumphini Park
PARK

1 ⊙ Map p100, G1

Named after the Buddha's birthplace in Nepal, central Bangkok's biggest and most popular park has nurtured many a bike rider, jogger, *đà·grôr* (a Thai ball game) player and t'ai chi practitioner – all best observed during the cool morning hours. Keep your eyes peeled for the enormous urban monitor lizards.

(สวนลุมพินี; bounded by Th Sarasin, Th Phra Ram IV, Th Witthayu/Wireless Rd & Th Ratchadamri; ⊙4.30am-9pm; ⏰; Ⓜ Lumphini exit 3, Si Lom exit 1, Ⓢ Sala Daeng exit 3, Ratchadamri exit 2)

Bangkokian Museum
MUSEUM

2 ⊙ Map p100, B2

This museum illustrates an often-overlooked period of Bangkok's history, the 1950s and '60s. The grounds consist of two handsome wooden homes, both of which are decked out with their original furniture, and an adjacent museum that is dedicated to local history. A visit takes the form of an informal guided tour in halting English, and photography is encouraged.

(พิพิธภัณฑ์ชาวบางกอก; 273 Soi 43, Th Charoen Krung; admission free; ⊙10am-4pm Wed-Sun; ⛴ Tha Si Phraya)

Kathmandu Photo Gallery
ART GALLERY

3 ⊙ Map p100, C3

Bangkok's only gallery wholly dedicated to photography is housed in an attractively restored Sino-Portuguese shophouse. The work of the owner, acclaimed Thai photographer Manit Sriwanichpoom, is on display on the ground floor, and the small, airy upstairs gallery plays host to changing exhibitions by local and international shooters.

(www.kathmandu-bkk.com; 87 Th Pan; admission free; ⊙11am-7pm Tue-Sun; Ⓢ Surasak exit 3)

Ruen-Nuad Massage Studio
MASSAGE

4 ⊙ Map p100, F3

Set in a refurbished wooden house, this charming place successfully skirts both the tackiness and New Age style that characterise most Bangkok massage joints. Prices are approachable, too.

(☎0 2632 2662; 42 Th Convent; massage per hour 350B; ⊙10am-9pm; Ⓜ Si Lom exit 2, Ⓢ Sala Daeng exit 2)

Queen Saovabha Memorial Institute
WILDLIFE

5 ⊙ Map p100, E1

This snake farm, one of only a few worldwide, was established in 1923 to breed snakes for antivenoms. There's a small on-site museum dedicated to snakes. Venom is collected during daily milkings (11am Monday to Friday), while daily snake-handling performances (2.30pm Monday to

AUSTIN BUSH / GETTY IMAGES ©

Kathmandu Photo Gallery

Friday, 11am Saturday and Sunday) are held at the outdoor amphitheatre. (สถานเสาวภา, Snake Farm; cnr Th Phra Ram IV & Th Henri Dunant; adult/child 200/50B; 9.30am-3.30pm Mon-Fri, to 1pm Sat & Sun; M Si Lom exit 1, S Sala Daeng exit 3)

Health Land
MASSAGE

6 Map p100, D4

This, the main branch of a long-established Thai massage empire, offers good-value, no-nonsense massage and spa treatments in a tidy environment. It's popular, so book your treatment or massage at least a day in advance. (0 2637 8883; www.healthlandspa.com; 120 Th Sathon Neua/North; massage 2hr 500B; 9am-9.30pm; S Surasak exit 3)

Sri Mariamman Temple
TEMPLE

7 Map p100, C3

Built by Tamil immigrants in the 1860s, this Hindu temple is a colourful place of worship in every sense of the word, from the multihued main temple to the eclectic range of people of many faiths and ethnicities who come to make offerings. Thais often call it Wat Khaek – *kàak* being a common expression for people of Indian descent. (วัดพระศรีมหาอุมาเทวี/วัดแขก, Wat Phra Si Maha Umathewi; cnr Th Silom & Th Pan; admission free; 6am-8pm; S Surasak exit 3)

MR Kukrit Pramoj House
HISTORIC BUILDING

8 ◎ Map p100, E4

Former Thai prime minister Mom Ratchawong Kukrit Pramoj once resided in this beautiful garden compound that today is open to visitors. European-educated but devoutly Thai, MR Kukrit surrounded himself with the best of both worlds: five traditional teak buildings, Thai art, Western books and lots of heady conversations. The grounds are sometimes booked out for events, so call before visiting.

(บ้านหม่อมราชวงศ์คึกฤทธิ์ปราโมช; ☏0 2286 8185; Soi 7/Phra Phinit, Th Narathiwat Ratchanakharin; adult/child 50/20B; ◷10am-4pm; ⓢ Chong Nonsi exit 2)

Oriental Spa
SPA

9 ◎ Map p100, A3

Regarded as among the premier spas in the world, the Oriental Spa sets the standard for Asian-style spa treatment. Depending on where you flew in from, the jet-lag massage might be a good option. All treatments require advance booking. The spa is located opposite the hotel, across Mae Nam Chao Phraya, and is accessible via a hotel shuttle boat.

(☏0 2659 9000, ext 7440; www.mandarin-oriental.com/bangkok/luxury-spa; Mandarin Oriental, 48 Soi 40, Th Charoen Krung; massage/spa packages from 2900B; ◷9am-10pm; ⚓Tha Oriental or hotel shuttle boat from Tha Sathon/Central Pier)

Silom Galleria
ART GALLERY

10 ◎ Map p100, B3

The only reason to visit this rather empty-feeling art- and jewellery-focused shopping centre is for a peek into some of Bangkok's better commercial art galleries, namely **Number 1 Gallery** (www.number1-gallery.com; ◷10am-7pm Mon-Sat), **Tang Gallery** (◷11am-7pm Mon-Sat), and **Thavibu Gallery** (www.thavibu.com; ◷11am-6pm Mon-Sat), which are located on the 4th and 5th floors, admission free.

(919/1 Th Silom; ◷11am-10pm; ⓢ Surasak exit 3)

Banyan Tree Spa
SPA

11 ◎ Map p100, G3

A combination of highly trained staff and high-tech facilities have provided this hotel spa with a glowing reputation. Come for unique signature treatments based on Thai traditions,

Top Tip

Art Attack

Bangkok is home to an ever-expanding network of private art galleries. To keep tabs, or see what recommended exhibitions are on during your stay, check out the **Bangkok Art Map** (www.facebook.com/bangkokartmap).

or the James Bond–esque 'Tranquility Hydro Mist'.

(☎ 0 2679 1052; www.banyantreespa.com; 21st fl, Banyan Tree Hotel, 21/100 Th Sathon Tai/South; massage packages from 3500B, spa packages from 6500B; ⊙9am-10pm; Ⓜ Lumphini exit 2)

H Gallery   ART GALLERY

12 Map p100, D3

Housed in a refurbished colonial-era wooden building, H is generally considered among the city's leading private galleries. It is also seen as a jumping-off point for Thai artists with international ambitions, such as Jakkai Siributr and Somboon Hormthienthong.

(www.hgallerybkk.com; 201 Soi 12, Th Sathon Neua/North; admission free; ⊙10am-6pm Wed-Sat, by appointment Tue; Ⓢ Chong Nonsi exit 1)

Neilson Hays Library   LIBRARY

13 Map p100, C2

The oldest English-language library in Thailand, the Neilson Hays dates back to 1922, and today remains the city's noblest place for a read – with the added benefit of air-con. It has a good selection of children's books and a decent selection of titles on Thailand. Nonmembers are expected to pay a 50B fee to use the facilities.

(www.neilsonhayslibrary.com; 195 Th Surawong; membership from 1900B; ⊙9.30am-5pm Tue-Sun; Ⓢ Surasak exit 3)

 Top Tip

Hotel Boats

Getting out on Mae Nam Chao Phraya is a great way to escape Bangkok's traffic, and to experience the city's maritime history. So it's fortunate that the city's riverside hotels also have some of the most attractive boats shuttling along the river (they are technically meant for the use of hotel guests, but staff don't generally ask too many questions). In most cases these free boat shuttle services run from Tha Sathon (also known as Central Pier) to their mother hotel, departing every 10 or 15 minutes. There's no squeeze, no charge and a uniformed crew member will help you get on and off the boat.

Eating

nahm   THAI $$$

14 Map p100, G3

Australian chef and cookbook author David Thompson is behind what is quite possibly the best Thai restaurant in Bangkok. Using ancient cookbooks as his inspiration, Thompson has given new life to previously extinct dishes such as 'smoked fish curry with prawns, chicken livers, cockles and black pepper'. If you're expecting bland gentrified Thai food that is meant for foreigners, prepare

to be disappointed. Reservations are highly recommended.
(📞0 2625 3388; www.comohotels.com/metropolitanbangkok/dining/nahm; ground fl, Metropolitan Hotel, 27 Th Sathon Tai/South; set lunch 1300B, set dinner 2000B, mains 260-700B; 🕙noon-2pm Mon-Fri, 7-10.30pm daily; Ⓜ Lumphini exit 2)

Eat Me

15 Map p100, F3   INTERNATIONAL $$$

The dishes offered on the menu at this lasting restaurant, with descriptions such as 'fig & blue cheese ravioli served with walnuts, rosemary and brown butter', or 'beef cheek tagine with saffron and dates', may sound all over the map or perhaps even somewhat pretentious, but they are actually just plain tasty. A buzzy, casual-yet-sophisticated atmosphere, great cocktails and a handsome wine list, and some of the city's best desserts, are additional reasons why this

is one of our favourite restaurants in Bangkok.
(📞0 2238 0931; www.eatmerestaurant.com; Soi Phiphat 2; mains 340-4500B; 🕙3pm-1am; 🖉; Ⓜ Si Lom exit 2, Ⓢ Sala Daeng exit 2)

Kai Thort Jay Kee

NORTHEASTERN THAI $$

16 Map p100, H1

Although the *sôm-dam* (spicy green papaya salad), sticky rice and *lâhp* (spicy 'salad' of minced meat) give the impression of a northeastern Thai eatery, the restaurant's namesake deep-fried bird is more southern in origin. Regardless, smothered in a thick layer of crispy deep-fried garlic, it is none other than a truly Bangkok experience.
(Soi Polo Fried Chicken; 137/1-3 Soi Sanam Khlii/Polo; mains 40-280B; 🕙11am-9pm; Ⓜ Lumphini exit 3)

Never Ending Summer

THAI $$

17 Map p100, A2

The cheesy name doesn't do justice to this surprisingly sophisticated Thai restaurant located in a former warehouse in a seemingly hidden compound by the river. Join Bangkok's beautiful and edgy crowd for anti-quated Thai dishes such as cubes of watermelon served with a dry 'dressing' of fish, sugar and deep-fried shallots, or fragrant green curry with pork and fresh bird's-eye-chilli.
(📞0 2861 0953; www.facebook.com/TheNeverEndingSummer; 41/5 Th Charoen Nakhon; mains 140-350B; 🕙11am-11pm; 🚢 river-crossing ferry from River City Pier)

☑ Top Tip

Reservations

If you have a lot of friends in tow or will be attending a formal restaurant (including hotel restaurants), reservations are recommended. Bookings are also recommended for Sunday brunches and dinner cruises. Otherwise, you generally won't have a problem scoring a table at the vast majority of restaurants in Bangkok.

Taling Pling
THAI $$

18 Map p100, C3

Long-standing Taling Pling has moved into more sophisticated digs in this low-rise 'community mall'. Luckily the menu remains the same, spanning largely seafood- and vegetable-based Thai dishes, including a handful made with the eponymous tart vegetable. Great for an upmarket-feeling Thai meal that doesn't skimp on flavour. (Baan Silom, Soi 19, Th Silom; mains 110-245B; ⏱11am-10pm; Ⓢ Surasak exit 3)

Muslim Restaurant
THAI-MUSLIM $

19 Map p100, B3

Plant yourself in one of the wooden booths of this ancient eatery for a glimpse into what restaurants in Bangkok used to be like. The menu, much like the interior design, doesn't appear to have changed much in the restaurant's 70-year history, and the biryanis, curries and samosas are still more Indian-influenced than Thai. (1354-6 Th Charoen Krung; mains 40-140B; ⏱6.30am-5.30pm; ☻Tha Oriental; Ⓢ Saphan Taksin exit 1)

Le Normandie
FRENCH $$$

20 Map p100, A3

For decades Le Normandie has been synonymous with fine dining in Bangkok. A revolving cast of Michelin-starred guest chefs and some of the world's most decadent ingredients keep up the standard; appropriately, formal attire

PETER UNGER / GETTY IMAGES ©

Moon Bar (p109)

(including jacket) is required. Book ahead. (☎0 2659 9000, ext 7670; www.mandarinoriental.com/bangkok/fine-dining/le-normandie; Mandarin Oriental, 48 Soi 40, Th Charoen Krung; mains 980-3750B; ⏱noon-2.30pm & 7-11pm Mon-Sat, 7-11pm Sun; ☻Tha Oriental or hotel shuttle boat from Tha Sathon/Central Pier)

Chennai Kitchen
INDIAN $

21 Map p100, C3

This thimble-sized mom-and-pop restaurant near the Hindu temple puts out some of the most solid southern Indian vegetarian food around. The yard-long *dosa* (a crispy southern Indian crêpe) is always a good choice, but if

Local Life
Dinner Cruises

Several companies run dinner cruises along Mae Nam Chao Phraya, and a one-stop centre for all your cruise needs is the **River City Information Desk** (Map p100, A2; ☎0 2639 4532, 0 2237 0077; www.river-city.co.th; ground fl, River City, 23 Th Yotha; ⓒ10am-10pm; 🚤Tha Si Phraya/River City or shuttle boat from Tha Sathon), where tickets can be purchased for **Grand Pearl** (☎0 2861 0255; www.grandpearlcruise.com; ⓒcruise 7.30-9.30pm), **Chao-phraya Cruise** (☎0 2541 5599; www.chaophrayacruise.com; ⓒcruise 7-9pm), **Wan Fah** (☎0 2622 7657; www.wanfah.in.th/eng/dinner; ⓒcruise 7-9pm), **Chao Phraya Princess** (☎0 2860 3700; www.thaicruise.com; ⓒcruise 7.45-9.45pm) and **White Orchid** (☎0 2476 5207; www.thairivercruise.com; ⓒcruise 7.45-9.45pm). Tickets range from 1500B to 1700B. Cruises last two hours and depart from River City Pier.

you're feeling indecisive (or exceptionally famished) go for the banana-leaf *thali*, which seems to incorporate just about everything in the kitchen. (107/4 Th Pan; mains 70-150B; ⓒ10am-3pm & 6-9.30pm; ▣; ⑤Surasak exit 3)

Dai Masu
JAPANESE $$

22 🍴 Map p100, E2

The emphasis at this cosy, retro-themed Japanese restaurant is on *ya-kiniku* (DIY grilled meat). But we also love the tasty, tiny sides ranging from

crispy spears of cucumber in a savoury marinade to a slightly bitter salad of paper-thin slices of eggplant. (www.facebook.com/shichirinizakayadaimasu; 9/3 Soi Than Tawan; dishes 49-300B; ⓒ11.30am-2pm & 6-11pm, to 10pm Sat & Sun; 🛜; Ⓜ Si Lom exit 2, ⑤ Sala Daeng exit 1)

Le Du
INTERNATIONAL $$$

23 🍴 Map p100, E3

The name a play on the Thai word for season, Le Du intertwines Thai dishes and Western flavours with, not surprisingly, an emphasis on fresh, seasonal ingredients. For the full experience, including some inventive desserts, come at dinnertime for the four- or seven-course tasting menus (990B to 1590B). (☎0 92919 9969; www.ledubkk.com; 399/3 Soi 7, Th Silom; mains 220-2900B; ⓒ11.30am-2.30pm & 6-11pm Mon-Fri, 6-11pm Sat; 🛜▣; ⑤Chong Nonsi exit 2)

Somboon Seafood
CHINESE-THAI $$$

24 🍴 Map p100, D2

Somboon is known for doing the best curry-powder crab in town. Another speciality is *Ƅlah grà·pohng nêung see·éw* (soy-steamed sea bass), which like all good Thai seafood, should be enjoyed with an immense platter of *kôw pàt Ƅoo* (fried rice with crab) and as many friends as you can pull together. (☎0 2233 3104; www.somboonseafood.com; cnr Th Surawong & Th Narathiwat Ratch-anakharin/Chong Nonsi; mains 120-900B; ⓒ4-11.30pm; ⑤Chong Nonsi exit 3)

Kalapapruek THAI $

25 Map p100, C3

This is the sort of restaurant where you're bound to encounter big-haired ladies and stiff silk suits – in Bangkok, tell-tale signs of a quality meal. The diverse menu spans regional Thai specialities from just about every region, daily specials and, occasionally, seasonal treats as well.

(27 Th Pramuan; mains 60-330B; ☺8am-6pm Mon-Sat, to 3pm Sun; S Surasak exit 3)

Sushi Tsukiji JAPANESE $$

26 Map p100, F2

Th Thaniya is home to many hostess bars catering to visiting Japanese, so naturally, the quality of the street's Japanese restaurants is high. Specialising in raw fish, dinner at Tsukiji – named after Tokyo's famous seafood market – is pricey, so come for lunch, when the restaurant serves sushi sets for as little as 198B.

(62/19-20 Th Thaniya; sushi per item 60-700B; ☺11am-2pm & 5.30-10.30pm; M Si Lom exit 2, S Sala Daeng exit 1)

Soi 10 Food Centres THAI $

27 Map p100, D2

These two adjacent buildings tucked behind Soi 10 are the main lunchtime stations for this area's office staff. Choices range from southern-style *kôw gaang* (point-and-choose curries ladled over rice) to virtually every incarnation of Thai noodle.

(Soi 10, Th Silom; mains 20-60B; ☺8am-2pm Mon-Fri; M Si Lom exit 2, S Sala Daeng exit 1)

Drinking

Moon Bar BAR

28 Map p100, G3

The Banyan Tree Hotel's Moon Bar kick-started the rooftop trend, and as Bangkok continues to grow at a mad pace, the view from 61 floors up only gets better. Arrive well before sunset and grab a coveted seat to the right of the bar for the most impressive views. Following the custom of Bangkok's nicer bars, shorts and/or sandals are not allowed.

(www.banyantree.com/en/web/banyantree/ap-thailand-bangkok/vertigo-and-moon-bar; 61st fl, Banyan Tree Hotel, 21/100 Th Sathon Tai/South; ☺5pm-1am; M Lumphini exit 2)

Smalls BAR

29 Map p100, F4

The kind of new bar that feels like it's been there forever, Smalls combines a cheekily decadent interior, an inviting rooftop and live music on Thursdays and Fridays. The eclectic house cocktails are strong, if sweet, and appropriately, bar snacks range from rillettes to quesadillas.

(186/3 Soi Suan Phlu; ☺8.30pm-late; M Lumphini exit 2 & taxi)

Namsaah Bottling Trust BAR

30 Map p100, D3

Namsaah is all about twists. From its home – a former mansion painted hot pink and decked out in a clubby vibe – to the cocktails – classics with a tweak or two – and the bar snacks and dishes –

think *pàt tai* with foie gras – everything's a little bit off in just the right way.
(www.namsaah.com; 401 Soi 7, Th Silom; Ⓜ Si Lom exit 2, Ⓢ Sala Daeng exit 2)

Vesper

BAR

31 Map p100, E2

One of the freshest faces on Bangkok's drinking scene is this deceptively classic-feeling bar. As the name suggests, the emphasis here is on cocktails, including several revived classics and mixed drinks mellowed by ageing for six weeks in white oak barrels.
(www.vesperbar.co; 10/15 Th Convent; ⏱ 11.30am-2.30pm & 5pm-midnight Mon-Thu, 11.30am-2.30pm & 5pm-1am Fri, 5pm-1pm Sat, 5pm-midnight Sun; Ⓜ Si Lom exit 2, Ⓢ Sala Daeng exit 2)

Maggie Choo's

BAR

32 Map p100, B3

A former bank vault with a Chinatown opium-den vibe, secret passageways and lounging women in silk dresses; with all this going on, it's easy to forget that the new Maggie Choo's is actually a bar. Creative cocktails and a crowd that blends selfie-snapping locals and curious tourists are reminders of this. Sunday nights see one of Bangkok's only gay nights at an otherwise hetero place.
(www.facebook.com/maggiechoos; basement, Novotel Bangkok Fenix Silom, 320 Th Silom; ⏱ 7.30pm-2am Sun-Thu, to 3am Fri & Sat; Ⓢ Surasak exit 1)

Hanakaruta

BAR

33 Map p100, D3

The floor-to-ceiling wall of bottles here is proof of Hanakaruta's dedication to booze. Sake and *shochu* are specialities, but we love the house-made *umeshu* (plum wine). There's a menu of bar snacks (60B to 680B) that, like the drinks, are served with Japanese efficiency.
(www.facebook.com/hanakaruta; Soi 10, Th Sathon Neua/North; ⏱ 6pm-2am Mon-Sat; Ⓢ Chong Nonsi exit 1)

Sky Bar

BAR

34 Map p100, B3

One of the highest alfresco bars in the world, Sky Bar, located on the 63rd floor of this upmarket restaurant compound, provides heart-stopping views over Mae Nam Chao Phraya. Note that the dress code doesn't allow access to those wearing shorts or sandals.
(www.lebua.com/sky-bar; 63rd fl, State Tower, 1055 Th Silom; ⏱ 6pm-1am; Ⓢ Saphan Taksin exit 3)

Tapas Room

CLUB

35 Map p100, E2

Although it sits staunchly at the front of Bangkok's pinkest street, this long-standing two-level disco manages to bring in just about everybody. Come from Thursday to Saturday, when Tapas features a combination of DJs and live percussion.
(114/17-18 Soi 4, Th Silom; ⏱ 7pm-2am; Ⓜ Si Lom exit 2, Ⓢ Sala Daeng exit 1)

Understand

Patpong

Super Pussy! Pussy Collection! The neon signs leave little doubt about the dominant industry in Patpong, the world's most infamous strip of go-go bars. There is enough skin on show in Patpong to make Hugh Hefner blush, and a trip to an upstairs club could mean you'll never look at a ping-pong ball or a dart the same way again.

Roots in 'R&R'

Patpong occupies two soi that run between Th Silom and Th Surawong in Bangkok's financial district. The streets are privately owned by – and named for – the Chinese-Thai Patpongpanich family, who bought the land in the 1940s and built Patpong Soi 1 and its shophouses; Soi 2 was laid later. During the Vietnam War the first bars and clubs opened to cater to American soldiers on 'R&R'. The scene grew through the '70s and peaked in the '80s, when official Thai tourism campaigns made the sort of 'sights' available in Patpong a pillar of their marketing.

Prostitution in Thailand

Prostitution is illegal in Thailand but there are as many as two million sex workers, the vast majority of whom – women and men – cater to Thai men. Many come from poorer regional areas, such as Isan in the northeast, while others might be students helping themselves through university. Sociologists suggest Thais often view sex through a less moralistic filter than Westerners. That doesn't mean Thai wives like their husbands using prostitutes, but it's only recently that the empowerment of women through education and employment has led to a more vigorous questioning of this very widespread practice.

Patpong Today

These days, Patpong has mellowed – somewhat. Thanks in part to the popular night market that fills the soi after 5pm, it draws so many tourists that it has become a sort of sex theme park. There are still plenty of the stereotypical middle-aged men ogling pole dancers, sitting in dark corners of the so-called 'blow-job bars' and paying 'bar fines' to take girls to hotels that charge by the hour. But you'll also be among other tourists and families who come to see what all the fuss is about.

Viva & Aviv

BAR

36 Map p100, A2

An enviable riverside location, with casual open-air seating and a funky atmosphere, makes this restaurant-ish bar a contender for Bangkok's best sunset-cocktail destination. Expect a punheavy menu (sample item: I 'foc'cat cia' name!) of pizzas, meaty snacks and salads that really is no joke.
(www.vivaaviv.com; ground fl, River City, 23 Th Yotha; ⊘11am-midnight; ⛴Tha Si Phraya/River City)

Ku Dé Ta

CLUB

37 Map p100, E3

The biggest new thing on Bangkok's club scene – literally and figuratively – the Bangkok branch of Ku Dé Ta spans several bars, two restaurants and a vast nightclub. Expect an entry fee of 500B after 10pm on Fridays and Saturdays.
(www.kudeta.com/bangkok; 38th & 39th fl, Sathorn Square Complex, 98 Th Sathon Neua/North; ⊘11am-1am Mon-Thu, to 3am Fri & Sat; ⓢChong Nonsi exit 1)

Wong's Place

BAR

38 Map p100, H3

Want to emulate the life of an in-the-know expat on a big night out? It's as easy as heading to Wong's, a legendarily divey drinking spot with an old-school soundtrack. Don't arrive before midnight, and good luck departing before the sun rises.
(27/3 Soi Si Bamphen; ⊘9pm-late Tue-Sun; ⓂLumphini exit 1)

Entertainment

Bamboo Bar

LIVE MUSIC

The Bamboo Bar at the Mandarin Oriental (see **20** Map p100, A3) is famous for its live lounge jazz, which holds court inside a colonial-era cabin of lazy fans, broad-leafed palms and rattan decor. Contact the bar ahead of time to see what artists are in residence during your visit.
(☎0 2236 0400; www.mandarinoriental.com/bangkok/fine-dining/the-bamboo-bar; ground fl, Mandarin Oriental, 48 Soi 40, Th Charoen Krung; ⊘11am-11.45pm Sun-Thu, to 12.45am Fri & Sat; ⛴Tha Oriental or hotel shuttle boat from Tha Sathon/Central Pier)

Sala Rim Naam

THEATRE

39 Map p100, A3

The historic Mandarin Oriental hosts a dinner theatre in a sumptuous Thai pavilion located across the river in Thonburi. The price is well above average, reflecting the means of the hotel's client base, and the performance gets positive reviews.
(☎0 2437 3080; www.mandarinoriental.com/bangkok/fine-dining/sala-rim-naam; Mandarin Oriental Hotel, Soi 40, Th Charoen Krung; tickets 2825B; ⊘dinner & show 8.15-9.30pm; ⛴Tha Oriental or hotel shuttle boat from Tha Sathon/Central Pier)

Patpong

RED-LIGHT DISTRICT

40 ⭐ Map p100, E2

Possibly one of the most famous
red-light districts in the world, today
any 'charm' that Patpong (p111)
used to possess has been eroded by
modern tourism – you will find that
fake Rolex watches and Diesel T-shirts
are more ubiquitous than flesh. If
you must, be sure to agree to the
price of entry and drinks before
taking a seat at one of Patpong's
1st-floor 'pussy shows', otherwise
you are highly likely to receive an
astronomical bill.
(Soi Patpong 1 & 2, Th Silom; ⏱4pm-2am;
Ⓜ Si Lom exit 2, Ⓢ Sala Daeng exit 1)

Patpong

Shopping

House of Chao

ANTIQUES

41 🔒 Map p100, D3

This three-storey antique shop, located
in an antique shophouse, has everything
necessary to deck out your fantasy
colonial-era mansion. Particularly interesting are the various weatherworn
doors and trellises that can be found in
the covered area behind the showroom.
(9/1 Th Decho; ⏱9.30am-7pm; Ⓢ Chong
Nonsi exit 3)

Everyday by Karmakamet

HANDICRAFTS

42 🔒 Map p100, F2

Part cafe, part showroom for the
eponymous brand's huge selection of
candles, incense, essential oils and
other fragrant and nonfragrant items,
Karmakamet is the ideal gift stop.
(Soi Yada; ⏱10am-10pm; Ⓜ Si Lom exit 2,
Ⓢ Sala Daeng exit 1)

River City

ANTIQUES

43 🔒 Map p100, A2

Only got time for one antique shop?
This four-storey complex of art and
antiques is a one-stop shop for a
Burmese Buddha image, black silk or
a *benjarong* (traditional royal Thai
ceramics) tea set, and you pay for the
quality. The stores can arrange to ship
your buys back home.
(www.rivercity.co.th; 23 Th Yotha; ⏱10am-
10pm; 🚢Tha Si Phraya/River City)

Jim Thompson

TEXTILES

44 Map p100, E2

This Jim Thompson is the largest shop of the business that was founded by the international promoter of Thai silk. It sells colourful silk handkerchiefs, place mats, wraps and cushions. The styles and motifs appeal to older, somewhat more conservative tastes.

(www.jimthompson.com; 9 Th Surawong; ⊙9am-9pm; MSi Lom exit 2, SSala Daeng exit 3)

Tamnan Mingmuang

HANDICRAFTS

45 Map p100, F2

As soon as you step through the doors of this museumlike shop, the earthy smell of dried grass and stained wood rushes to meet you. Rattan, *yahn lí·pow* (a fernlike vine), water hyacinth woven into silklike patterns, and coconut shells carved into delicate bowls are among the exquisite pieces here that will outlast the souvenirs available on the streets.

(2nd fl, Thaniya Plaza, Th Thaniya; ⊙11am-8pm; MSi Lom exit 2, SSala Daeng exit 1)

OTOP Walking Street

MARKET

46 Map p100, B3

The strip of concrete that is situated under an expressway has been converted into an open-air market that sells regional Thai food, handicrafts and clothing, which are all made under the auspices of this eponymous government initiative. Open every day, but at its best on Tuesdays and Wednesdays, when the number of vendors increases and commerce is joined by traditional Thai performances.

(Phayathai-Bangkok Expressway; ⊙11am-9pm; SSaphan Taksin exit 1)

Understand

7-Eleven 4 Ever

Be extremely wary of any appointment that involves the words 'meet me at 7-Eleven'. In Bangkok alone, there are 2700 branches of 7-Eleven (known as *sair·wên* in Thai) – nearly a third the number found in all of North America. In central Bangkok, 7-Elevens are so ubiquitous that it's not uncommon to see two branches staring at each other from across the street. Although the company reports that its stores carry more than 2000 items, the fresh flavours of Thai cuisine are not reflected in the wares of a typical Bangkok 7-Eleven, the food selections of which are even junkier than those of its counterparts in the West. As in all shops in Thailand, alcohol is only available from 11am to 2pm and 5pm to midnight, and branches of 7-Eleven located near hospitals, temples and schools do not sell alcohol or cigarettes at all.

Lin & Sons Jewellers

JEWELLERY

47 Map p100, B3

Lin might be a bit pricier than your average Bangkok silver shop, but you know you're getting the genuine article. Available are classic pieces like silver chokers, thick bangles and custom-engraved cuff links.
(12/2 Soi 40, Th Charoen Krung; ⏰9am-6.30pm Mon-Sat; 🚤Tha Oriental)

Maison Des Arts

HANDICRAFTS

48 Map p100, B3

Hand-hammered, stainless-steel tableware occupies this warehouse retail shop. The bold style of the flatware dates back centuries and staff apply no pressure to indecisive shoppers.
(1334 Th Charoen Krung; ⏰11am-6pm Mon-Sat; 🚤Tha Oriental)

Thai Home Industries

HANDICRAFTS

49 Map p100, A3

Not your average Bangkok souvenir shop; a visit to this enormous traditional Thai building is a lot like picking around an abandoned attic of traditional Thai booty. The staff leave you to your own devices to poke around the bronzeware, silverware (especially cutlery) and other unexpected knick-knacks.
(35 Soi 40, Th Charoen Krung; ⏰9am-6.30pm Mon-Sat; 🚤Tha Oriental)

Top Tip

Counterfeits

Bangkok is ground zero for the production and sale of counterfeit goods. Although the prices may be enticing, keep in mind that counterfeit goods are almost always as shoddy as they are cheap.

Chiang Heng

ACCESSORIES

50 Map p100, B4

In need of a handmade stainless-steel wok or a manually operated coconut-milk strainer? Then we suggest you stop by this third-generation family-run kitchen-supply shop. Even if your cabinets are already stocked, a visit here is a glance into the type of specialised shops that have all but disappeared from Bangkok. There's no English-language sign; look for the blue wooden doors.
(1466 Th Charoen Krung; ⏰10.30am-7pm; ⓈSaphan Taksin exit 3)

Patpong Night Market

SOUVENIRS

51 Map p100, E2

You'll be faced with the competing distractions of strip-clubbing and shopping on this infamous street. And true to the area's illicit leanings, pirated goods make an appearance amid the largely wholesome crowd of families. Bargain with determination, as first-quoted prices tend to be astronomically high.
(Soi Patpong 1 & 2, Th Silom; ⏰6pm-midnight; Ⓜ Si Lom exit 2, Ⓢ Sala Daeng exit 1)

Local Life
RCA (Royal City Avenue)

Getting There

Ⓜ **MRT** Phra Ram 9 exit 3 and taxi.

The strip of dance clubs, live-music bars and pubs known as RCA (Royal City Avenue) has long been the first nightlife destination of choice for many young locals. However, in recent years, the clientele has grown up, and today RCA hosts visitors of just about any age, and a similarly diverse spread of venues to match.

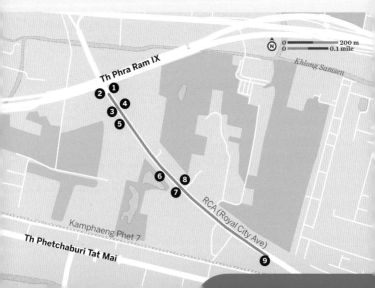

❶ Mama Noodle Stall

This late-night **stall** (RCA, off Th Phra Ram IX; ⏱9pm-2am) does a brisk trade in Thailand's most beloved instant noodle – here pimped out with real broth, vegetables and seafood.

❷ Slim/Onyx

Call it an education in clubbing: **Slim** (www.facebook.com/slimbkk; 29/22-32 RCA, off Th Phra Ram IX; admission 400B; ⏱9pm-2am), with its Top 40 soundtrack, is the entry-level course, while a visit next door to **Onyx** (onyxbangkok.com/home/th/; Royal City Ave/RCA, off Th Phra Ram IX; admission from 500B; ⏱8pm-late), with its EDM and late closing hours, will earn you a graduate degree.

❸ Route 66

Route 66 (www.route66club.com; 29/33-48 RCA, off Th Phra Ram IX; admission 300B; ⏱8pm-2am) has been around almost as long as RCA, but still manages to pull massive crowds. Top 40/hip hop rules the main space, but the compound's other 'levels' feature everything from Thai pop to live music.

❹ Patisserie Mori Osaka

The Japanese pedigree may confuse some, but **Patisserie Mori Osaka** (www.facebook.com/patisseriemoriosaka; RCA, off Th Phra Ram IX; pastries 90-130B; ⏱11am-10pm) actually does some of the better Western-style pastries in Bangkok.

❺ Castro

Coyote boys (topless dancers), late hours and a dark lounge: RCA's biggest gay **club** (www.facebook.com/Castro.rca.bangkok; RCA, off Th Phra Ram IX; admission 180B; ⏱9.30pm-2am) has all the essentials for a night you might live to regret.

❻ Vesbar

This Vespa-themed **bar** (www.facebook.com/GoVesBar; RCA, off Th Phra Ram IX; ⏱11am-midnight) serves up international dishes, import beers, and jazzy live music (Wednesdays, Fridays and Saturdays).

❼ Taksura

Existing somewhere between restaurant and pub is retro-themed **Taksura** (RCA, off Th Phra Ram IX; ⏱6pm-2am). If you're fuelling up for the clubs, the spicy *gàp glâam* (Thai drinking snacks) won't disappoint.

❽ Rehab

The beats and bright lights of EDM not your thing? Prefer craft beer to vodka shots? Then head to this cosy **bar** (www.facebook.com/rehabrca; RCA, off Th Phra Ram IX; ⏱5.30pm-2am) with an emphasis on live blues and jazz music.

❾ House

House (www.houserama.com; 3rd fl, RCA Plaza, RCA, off Th Phra Ram IX) is Bangkok's first art-house cinema, and shows lots of non-Hollywood foreign flicks.

Explore

Sukhumvit

Japanese enclaves, French restaurants, Middle Eastern nightlife zones, tacky 'sex-pat' haunts: it's all here along Th Sukhumvit, Bangkok's unofficial international zone. Where temples and suburban rice fields used to be, today you'll find shopping centres, nightlife and a host of other tidy amenities that cater to resident and visiting foreigners, and middle-class Thais.

KWANCHAI_K PHOTOGRAPHY / GETTY IMAGES ©

The Sights in a Day

☀️ Begin your day with a swing through **Khlong Toey Market** (p122), central Bangkok's largest and most hectic market. Afterwards, ride the MRT to the significantly more sedate Thai house museum, **Kamthieng House** (p122).

☀️ Take advantage of Sukhumvit's spread of international cuisines and have a Middle Eastern lunch at **Nasir Al-Masri** (p125). Get fitted for a suit at one of the nearby tailors, such as **Raja's Fashions** (p134). Wind down with a Thai-style massage at **Coran** (p129) or **Asia Herb Association** (p129).

🌙 Kick the evening off with cocktails and art at **WTF** (p128). For dinner, consider upscale Thai at **Bo.lan** (p123) or sublime Japanese at **Jidori-Ya Kenzou** (p122). Continue with live music at **Living Room** (p132) or **Titanium** (p132), followed by booty-shaking at **Grease** (p130) or one of the clubs at **Arena 10** (p131).

 Best of Bangkok

Ethnic Cuisine
Jidori-Ya Kenzou (p122)

Nasir Al-Masri (p125)

Dance Clubs
Grease (p130)

Arena 10 (p131)

Glow (p131)

Quirky Souvenirs
Shop @ TCDC (p134)

ZudRangMa Records (p134)

Thai Massage
Asia Herb Association (p129)

Live Music
Titanium (p132)

Living Room (p132)

Fine Dining
Little Beast (p122)

For Kids
Bo.lan (p123)

Getting There

Ⓢ **BTS** Nana, Asok, Phrom Phong, Thong Lo and Ekkamai.

Ⓜ **MRT** Khlong Toei, Queen Sirikit National Convention Centre and Sukhumvit.

A
B
C
D

1

Soi 3 (Nana Nua)
Soi 3/1
28
31
Soi 5
Soi 7
Soi 11
Soi 13
Soi 15
Soi 21 (Asoke)
Soi 23
Soi Prasanmit

8

34

Chalerm Mahanakhon Expwy

Soi 2

Soi 4 (Nana Tai)
Soi 6
Soi 7/1
Nana S
24
37

39

2

Chuvit Garden
Soi 8
Soi 10
9
30
Soi 19
Kamthieng House **1**
26
Soi 23
Sukhumvit **33**
36 **27**

38 M
Asok S
Soi Cowboy

Soi 12
Soi 14
Soi 25
Soi 27
Th Sukhumvit
23
Soi 31
Soi 31/1
Soi 33
Soi 33/1

3

Soi 16
Soi 18
11
29
13

Th Ratchadaphisek

Lake Ratchada

Benjakiti Park

Soi 20
Soi 22
Benjasiri Park **35**
Phrom Phong S

3

Soi 24

4

Soi 10

KHLONG TOEY

Soi 26

Queen Sirikit National Convention Centre M

Khlong Toei M

5

Th Phra Ram IV
Khlong Toei Market **2**

10

For reviews see

- ⊙ Sights — p122
- ✕ Eating — p122
- 🍷 Drinking — p128
- ★ Entertainment — p132
- 🛍 Shopping — p134

Khlong Saen Saeb

Ⓝ 0 — 500 m
0 — 0.25 miles

Soi 39

Soi Ekamai 21

19
16

Soi Phrom Si 2

Soi Prom Si 1

40
Soi 49/9

18 Soi Thong Lor 16

Soi Thong Lor 13

Soi Thong Lor 15

Soi Thong Lor 12

4

Soi Thong Lor 10 (Soi Ekamai 5)

32

25

Soi 49

Soi Prommit

21

Soi 39

Soi 63 (Ekamai)

14

Soi Thong Lor 7

Soi 55 (Thong Lor)

Soi 45

Soi 49

Soi 51

6

20 Soi Thong Lor 5

Soi Ekamai 10

17

Th Sukhumvit

12
22

Soi 53

5

Soi Thong Lor 1

7

Soi Ekamai 6

Soi Ekamai 4

Ⓢ Thong Lo

15

Soi 36

Soi 38

Soi Ekamai 2

Eastern Bus Terminal — Ⓜ Ekkamai

Sights

Kamthieng House
MUSEUM

1 Map p120, C2

An engaging house museum, Kamthieng House transports visitors to a northern Thai village that is complete with informative displays of daily rituals, folk beliefs and everyday household chores, all within the setting of a traditional wooden house. This museum is operated by and shares space with the Siam Society, the publisher of the renowned *Journal of the Siam Society*, as well as a valiant preserver of traditional Thai culture.

(บ้านคำเที่ยง; Siam Society, 131 Soi 21/Asoke, Th Sukhumvit; adult/child 100B/free; ⏰9am-5pm Tue-Sat; **M**Sukhumvit exit 1, **S**Asok exit 3 or 6)

Top Tip
Decoding the Soi

All odd-numbered soi branching off Th Sukhumvit head north, while even numbers run south. Unfortunately, they don't line up sequentially (eg Soi 11 lies directly opposite Soi 8, Soi 39 is opposite Soi 26). Also, some larger soi are better known by alternative names, such as Soi 3/Nana Neua, Soi 21/Asoke, Soi 55/Thong Lor and Soi 63/Ekamai.

Khlong Toey Market
MARKET

2 Map p120, B5

This wholesale market, one of the city's largest, is inevitably the origin of many of the meals you'll eat during your stay in Bangkok. Although some corners of the market can't exactly be described as photogenic, you'll still want to bring a camera to capture the cheery fishmongers and stacks of durians. Get there early, ideally before 9am.

(ตลาดคลองเตย; cnr Th Ratchadaphisek & Th Phra Ram IV; ⏰5-10am; **M**Khlong Toei exit 1)

Eating

Jidori-Ya Kenzou
JAPANESE $$$

3 Map p120, D4

This cosy Japanese restaurant does excellent tofu dishes, delicious salads, and even desserts; basically everything here is above average, but the highlight is the smoky, perfectly seasoned chicken skewers. One of our favourite restaurants in Bangkok.

(off Soi 26, Th Sukhumvit; dishes 60-350B; ⏰5pm-midnight Mon-Sat; **S**Phrom Phong exit 4)

Little Beast
INTERNATIONAL $$$

4 Map p120, F3

With influences stemming from modern American cuisine, Little Beast isn't very Bangkok, but it is very good. Expect meaty mains, satisfying salads

Khlong Toey Market

and some of the best desserts in town (the ice-cream sandwiches alone are worth a trip).

(📞 0 2185 2670; www.facebook.com/little-beastbar; 44/9-10 Soi Thong Lor 13; mains 300-750B; ⏱5.30pm-1am Tue-Sat, 11am-4pm Sun; 🛜; Ⓢ Phrom Phong exit 3 & taxi)

Bo.lan
THAI $$$

 5 Ⓧ Map p120, F4

Bo and Dylan (Bo.lan, a play on words that also means 'ancient') have provided Bangkok with a compelling reason to reconsider upscale Thai cuisine. The couple's scholarly approach to cooking takes the form of seasonal set meals featuring antiquated dishes you're not

likely to find elsewhere. Reservations recommended.

(📞 0 2260 2962; www.bolan.co.th; 24 Soi 53, Th Sukhumvit; set meals 380-2280B; ⏱12.30-2.30pm & 7-10.30pm Thu-Sun, 6-10.30pm Tue-Wed; 🍴; Ⓢ Thong Lo exit 1)

Quince
INTERNATIONAL $$$

6 Ⓧ Map p120, E4

Back in 2011 Quince made an audible splash in Bangkok's dining scene with its retro-industrial interior and eclectic, internationally influenced menu. The formula has since been copied ad nauseam, but Quince continues to put out the type of vibrant, full-flavoured dishes, many with palpable Middle Eastern or Spanish influences, that

Understand
What's a Wát?

Bangkok is home to hundreds of wáts, temple compounds that have traditionally been at the centre of community life.

Buildings & Structures
Even the smallest wát will usually have a *bòht*, a *wí·hǎhn* and monks' living quarters.

Bòht The most sacred prayer room at a wát, often similar in size and shape to the *wí·hǎhn*. Aside from the fact it does not house the main Buddha image, you'll know the *bóht* because it is usually more ornately decorated and has eight cornerstones to mark its boundary.

Chedi (stupa) A large bell-shaped tower usually containing five structural elements symbolising (from bottom to top) earth, water, fire, wind and void; depending on the wát, relics of the Buddha, a Thai king or some other notable are housed inside.

Drum Tower Elevates the ceremonial drum beaten by novices.

Hǒr đrai The manuscript library: a structure for holding Buddhist scriptures. As these texts were previously made from palm leaves, *hǒr đrai* were typically elevated or built over water to protect them from flooding and/or termites.

Mon·dòp An open-sided, square building with four arches and a pyramidal roof, used to worship religious objects or texts.

ʼbrahng A towering phallic spire of Khmer origin serving the same religious purpose as a *chedi*.

Sǎh·lah (sala) A pavilion, often open-sided, for relaxation, lessons or miscellaneous activities.

Wí·hǎhn (vihara) The sanctuary for the temple's main Buddha image and where laypeople come to make their offerings. Classic architecture typically has a three-tiered roof representing the triple gems: the Buddha (the teacher), Dharma (the teaching) and Sangha (the followers).

made it stand out in the first place.
Reservations recommended.
(📞 0 2662 4478; www.quincebangkok.com;
Soi 45, Th Sukhumvit; mains 250-1800B;
🕙 11.30am-midnight; 🍴; Ⓢ Phrom Phong
exit 3)

Soul Food Mahanakorn   THAI $$$

7 🍴 Map p120, F4

Soul Food gets its interminable
buzz from its dual nature as both an
inviting restaurant – the menu spans
tasty interpretations of rustic Thai
and Southeast Asian dishes – and a
bar serving deliciously boozy, Thai-
influenced cocktails. Reservations
recommended.
(📞 0 2714 7708; www.soulfoodmahanakorn.
com; 56/10 Soi 55/Thong Lor, Th Sukhumvit;
mains 150-300B; 🕙 5.30pm-midnight; 🍴;
Ⓢ Thong Lo exit 3)

Nasir Al-Masri   MIDDLE EASTERN $$$

8 🍴 Map p120, A1

One of several Middle Eastern restaurants on Soi 3/1, Nasir Al-Masri is
easily recognisable by its thoroughly
impressive floor-to-ceiling stainless
steel 'theme'. Middle Eastern food
generally means meat, meat and
more meat, but there are also several
delicious vegie-based meze (small
dishes).
(4/6 Soi 3/1, Th Sukhumvit; mains 160-370B;
🕙 24hr; 🍴; Ⓢ Nana exit 1)

Myeong Ga   KOREAN $$$

9 🍴 Map p120, B2

Located on the ground floor of
Sukhumvit Plaza (the multistorey
complex also known as Korean Town),
this restaurant is the city's best destination for authentic Seoul food. Go for
the tasty prepared dishes or, if you've
got a bit more time, the excellent, DIY
Korean-style barbecue.
(ground fl, Sukhumvit Plaza, cnr Soi 12 & Th
Sukhumvit; mains 200-950B; 🕙 11am-10pm
Tue-Sun, 4-10pm Mon; Ⓜ Sukhumvit exit 3,
Ⓢ Asok exit 2)

Tenkaichi Yakiton
Nagiya   JAPANESE $$

10 🍴 Map p120, D5

Originating in Tokyo, this equal
parts cosy and hectic eatery is one
of Bangkok's best and most popular *izakaya* (Japanese tavern-style
restaurants). The highlights here are
the warming *nabe* (do-it-yourself

Ⓠ Local Life
Ethnic Cuisine

Sukhumvit's various ethnic enclaves are the logical destination
if you're growing weary of rice and
spice. Known colloquially as Little
Arabia, Soi 3/1 is home to several
Middle Eastern restaurants, while
a handful of Korean restaurants
can be found at Soi 12, and several
Japanese restaurants are located
around BTS Phrom Phong.

hotpots) and the smoky *yakitoshi* (grilled skewers of meat). Expect lots of Japanese-style welcoming – some might call it shouting – by the staff, and on weekends, a queue. (www.nagiya.com; Nihonmachi 105, 115 Soi 26, Th Sukhumvit; mains 90-160B; ⏰5pm-midnight; **S**Phrom Phong exit 1 & taxi)

Local Life
Sunday Brunch

Sunday brunch has become a Bangkok institution – particularly among the city's expat community – and the hotels along Th Sukhumvit offer some of the best spreads.

Rang Mahal (Map p120, C3; ⏰0 2261 7100; www.rembrandtbkk.com/dining/rang-mahal.htm; 26th fl, Rembrandt Hotel, 19 Soi 20, Th Sukhumvit; buffet 850B; ⏰11am-2.30pm Sun; 🍴; **M**Sukhumvit exit 2, **S**Asok exit 6) This Indian buffet is one of the most popular Sunday destinations for Bangkok's South Asian expat community.

Sunday Jazzy Brunch (Map p120, B2; ⏰0 2649 8888; www.sheratongrande-sukhumvit.com/sundayjazzybrunch; 1st fl, Sheraton Grande Sukhumvit, 250 Th Sukhumvit; adult 2320-3470B, child 1210B; ⏰noon-3pm Sun; 🍴; **M**Sukhumvit exit 3, **S**Asok exit 2) The Sheraton's Sunday brunch unites all the hotel's restaurant outlets to a soundtrack of live jazz.

Marriott Café (Map p120, A1; ⏰0 2656 7700; ground fl, JW Marriott, 4 Soi 2, Th Sukhumvit; buffet 1990B; ⏰11.30am-2.30pm Sun; 🍴; **S**Nana exit 3) The weekend brunch at this American hotel chain is likened to Thanksgiving year-round.

Bei Otto GERMAN $$$

11 Map p120, C3

Claiming a Bangkok residence for nearly 30 years, Bei Otto's major culinary bragging point is its pork knuckles, reputedly the best in town. A good selection of German beers and an attached delicatessen with brilliant breads and super sausages makes it even more attractive to go Deutsch. (www.beiotto.com; 1 Soi 20, Th Sukhumvit; mains 185-698B; ⏰11am-midnight; 🍴; **M**Sukhumvit exit 2, **S**Asok exit 4)

Opposite Mess Hall INTERNATIONAL $$$

12 Map p120, F4

Much like the dishes it serves (example: 'savoury duck waffle, leg confit, pate, crispy skin & piccalilli relish'), Opposite can be a bit hard to pin down. But how can you go wrong with a beautiful space, friendly service and excellent cocktails? There's a menu, but the best strategy is to see what the daily specials blackboard has to offer. (⏰0 2662 6330; www.oppositebangkok.com; 2nd fl, 27/2 Soi 51, Th Sukhumvit; dishes 120-650B; ⏰6.30-10.30pm Tue-Sat, noon-2pm & 6.30-10.30pm Sun; 🍴; **S**Thong Lo exit 1)

Sukhumvit street-food stall

Saras

INDIAN $

13 Map p120, C3

Order at the counter to be rewarded with crispy *dosa* (southern Indian crêpes), regional set meals or rich curries; dishes are brought to your table. There are shelves of Punjabi sweets and *chaat* (sweet and savoury snacks), and perhaps most endearingly, chai is served in earthenware cups. If only all fast food could be this satisfying.

(www.saras.co.th; Soi 20, Th Sukhumvit; mains 90-200B; ⏰9am-10.30pm; 🥄; Ⓜ Sukhumvit exit 2, Ⓢ Asok exit 4)

Supanniga Eating Room

THAI $$

14 Map p120, G3

Following the current trend of serving regional Thai food in an upmarket setting, this attractive eatery does a menu of unique dishes, many culled from Thailand's western provinces. It's not all about image, though, and the obscure Thai-style dips, tart salads and rich curries – including an entire vegetarian menu – deliver.

(www.supannigaeatingroom.com; 160/11 Soi 55/Thong Lor, Th Sukhumvit; mains 120-580B; ⏰11.30am-2.30pm & 5.30-11.30pm; 🥄; Ⓢ Thong Lo exit 3 & taxi)

Top Tip

Tipping

You shouldn't be surprised to learn that the tipping custom that is followed in Thailand is not as exact as it is in Japan (tip no one) or the USA (tip everyone). Thailand falls somewhere in between those two extremes, and some areas are left open to interpretation. Some people will leave roughly 10% tip at any sit-down restaurant where someone fills their glass every time they take a sip. Others don't. Most upmarket restaurants will apply a 10% service charge to the bill. Some patrons leave extra on top of the service charge, while others do not. The choice is entirely yours.

Soi 38
Night Market   THAI $

15 Map p120, F5

After a hard night of clubbing on Th Sukhumvit, head to this small but beloved convocation of open-air food vendors. If you're going sober, stick to the knot of 'famous' stalls tucked into an alley on the right side as you enter the street, or the excellent burgers at Daniel Thaiger.
(Soi 38, Th Sukhumvit; mains 30-60B; ☺8pm-3am; S Thong Lo exit 4)

Drinking

WTF   BAR

Located near Studio Lam (see 22 Map p120, F4), Wonderful Thai Friendship (what did you think it stood for?) is a funky and friendly neighbourhood bar that also packs in a gallery space. Arty locals and resident foreigners come for the old-school cocktails, live music and DJ events, poetry readings, art exhibitions and tasty bar snacks. And we, like them, give WTF our vote for Bangkok's best pub.
(www.wtfbangkok.com; 7 Soi 51, Th Sukhumvit; ☺6pm-1am Tue-Sun; S Thong Lo exit 3)

Tuba   BAR

16 Map p120, H2

Part storage room for over-the-top vintage furniture, part restaurant, part friendly local boozer, this quirky bar certainly doesn't lack in diversity, or fun. Indulge in a whole bottle (they'll hold onto it if you don't finish it) and don't miss the moreish chicken wings or the delicious deep-fried *lâhp* (spicy 'salad' of minced meat).
(34 Room 11-12 A, Soi Thong Lor 20/Soi Ekamai 21; ☺11am-2am; S Ekkamai exit 1 & taxi)

Mikkeller   BAR

17 Map p120, H4

These buzz-generating Danish 'gypsy' brewers have set up shop in Bangkok, granting us more than 30 beers on tap. Expect brews ranging from the local (Sukhumvit Brown Ale) to the insane (Beer Geek, a 13% alcohol oatmeal stout), an inviting atmosphere and good bar snacks.

(www.mikkellerbangkok.com; 26 Yaek 2, Soi Ekamai 10; ⏰5pm-midnight; Ⓢ Ekkamai exit 1 & taxi)

Badmotel
BAR

18 Map p120, G2

Badmotel blends the modern and the kitschy, the cosmopolitan and the Thai, in a way that has struck a nerve among Bangkok hipsters. This is manifest in drinks that combine Hale's Blue Boy, a Thai childhood drink staple, with rum and Thai dessert toppings, and bar snacks such as *naam prik ong* (a northern-style dip), here served with pappadams.

(www.facebook.com/badmotel; Soi 55/Thong Lor, Th Sukhumvit; ⏰5pm-1.30am; Ⓢ Thong Lo exit 3 & taxi)

Sugar Ray
BAR

19 Map p120, H2

Run by a team of fun Thai dudes who make flavoured syrups, Sugar Ray is a fun, funky hidden bar serving fun, funky cocktails; think an Old Fashioned made with aged rum, orange and cardamom syrup, and garnished with a piece of caramelised bacon.

(www.facebook.com/pages/Sugar-Ray-Youve-Just-Been-Poisoned/234918586711793; off Soi Ekamai 21; ⏰8pm-2am Wed, Fri & Sat; Ⓢ Ekkamai exit 1 & taxi)

J. Boroski Mixology
BAR

20 Map p120, F4

The eponymous mixologist here has done away with both addresses and cocktail menus to arrive at the modern equivalent of the speakeasy. Tell the boys behind the bar what flavours

Local Life
Spa Central

Th Sukhumvit is home to many of Bangkok's most recommended and reputable spas and massage studios, including the following:

Asia Herb Association (Map p120, F4; ☏0 2392 3631; www.asiaherbassociation .com; 58/19-25 Soi 55/Thong Lor, Th Sukhumvit; Thai massage per hour 400B; Thai massage with herbal compress 1½hr 900B; ⏰9am-2am; Ⓢ Thong Lo exit 3) This chain specialises in massage using *prà·kóp*, compresses filled with 18 different herbs.

Coran (Map p120, H4; ☏0 2726 9978; www.coranbangkok.com; 94-96/1 Soi Ekamai 10, Soi 63/Ekamai, Th Sukhumvit; Thai massage per hour 600B; ⏰11am-10pm; Ⓢ Ekkamai exit 4 & taxi) A classy, low-key spa housed in a Thai villa.

Divana Massage & Spa (Map p120, C2; ☏0 2261 6784; www.divanaspa.com; 7 Soi 25, Th Sukhumvit; massage from 1100B, spa packages from 2350B; ⏰11am-11pm Mon-Fri, 10am-11pm Sat-Sun; Ⓜ Sukhumvit exit 2, Ⓜ Asok exit 6) Divana retains a unique Thai touch, with a private setting in a garden house.

Top Tip
Opening Hours

Since 2004 authorities have ordered most of Bangkok's bars and clubs to close by 1am. A complicated zoning system sees venues in designated 'entertainment areas', including RCA, Th Silom and parts of Th Sukhumvit, open until 2am, but even these 'later' licences are subject to police whimsy.

you fancy and, using top-shelf liquor and unique ingredients, they'll create something individual and memorable. Located in an unmarked street near Soi Thong Lor 7; for exact location, refer to website.
(www.josephboroski.com; off Soi 55/Thong Lor, Th Sukhumvit; ⊙7pm-2am; 🛜; 🅂Thong Lo exit 3 & taxi)

Grease

CLUB

 21 Map p120, F3

Bangkok's newest, hottest nightclub is also one of its biggest – you could get lost in the four floors of dining venues, lounges and dance floors here.
(www.greasebangkok.com; 46/12 Soi 49, Th Sukhumvit; ⊙6pm-2am Mon-Sat; 🅂Phrom Phong exit 3 & taxi)

Studio Lam

BAR

22 Map p120, F4

An extension of uber-hip record label ZudRangMa, this new venue has a

Jamaican-style sound system custom-built for world and retro-Thai DJ sets and the occasional live show. Studio Lam is also one of the only indoor places in Bangkok to try *yah dorng*, traditional Thai-style herbal alcohol.
(www.facebook.com/studiolambangkok; Soi 51, Th Sukhumvit; ⊙6pm-1am Tue-Sun; 🅂Thong Lo exit 3)

Walden

BAR

 23 Map p120, D2

Get past the hyperminimalist/Kinfolk vibe, and the thoughtful Japanese touches at this new bar make it one of the more welcoming places in town. Come for a brief menu of drinks that spans Japanese-style 'highballs' to craft beers from the US, and simple, delicious bar snacks.
(7/1 Soi 31, Th Sukhumvit; ⊙6.30pm-1am Mon-Sat; 🅂Phrom Phong exit 5)

Cheap Charlie's

BAR

24 Map p120, B1

You're bound to have a mighty difficult time convincing your Thai friends to go to Th Sukhumvit only to sit at an outdoor wooden shack decorated with buffalo skulls and wagon wheels. Fittingly, Charlie's draws a staunchly foreign crowd that doesn't mind a bit of kitsch and sweat with its Singha.
(Soi 11, Th Sukhumvit; ⊙4.30-11.45pm Mon-Sat; 🅂Nana exit 3)

INGOLF POMPE / LOOK-FOTO / GETTY IMAGES ©

Q Bar (p132)

Arena 10 CLUB

25 Map p120, G3

This open-air entertainment zone is the destination of choice for Bangkok's young and beautiful – for the moment at least. **Demo** (www. facebook.com/demobangkok; admission free; ⏱9pm-2am) combines blasting beats and a NYC warehouse vibe, while **Funky Villa** (www.facebook.com/funky-villabkk; ⏱7pm-2am), with its outdoor seating and Top 40 soundtrack, is more chilled.
(Soi Thong Lor 10/Soi Ekamai 5; **S** Ekkamai exit 2 & taxi)

Glow CLUB

26 Map p120, C2

This self-proclaimed 'boutique' club starts things early in the evenings as a lounge that boasts an impressive spectrum of vodkas. As the evening progresses, enjoy tunes ranging from

☑ Top Tip
Smoking
Smoking has been outlawed at all indoor (and some quasi-outdoor) entertainment places since 2008.

Local Life

Club Alley

The streets that extend from Th Sukhumvit are home to many of Bangkok's most popular clubs. Ravers of university age tend to head to Soi 63/Ekamai, while the pampered elite play at Soi 55/Thong Lor, and expats and tourists tend to gravitate towards the clubs on Soi 11.

hip hop (Fridays) to electronica (Saturday) and everything in between. (www.glowbkk.com; 96/415 Soi Prasanmit; admission from 350B; ⊙10pm-1am Mon-Tue, to 2am Wed-Sat; M Sukhumvit exit 2, S Asok exit 3)

Narz

CLUB

27 Map p120, C2

Like a small clubbing neighbourhood, Narz consists of three vast zones boasting an equally vast variety of music. It's largely a domestic scene, but the odd guest DJ can pull a large crowd. (www.narzclubbangkok.net; 112 Soi 23; admission from 400B; ⊙9pm-2am; M Sukhumvit exit 2, S Asok exit 3)

Q Bar

CLUB

28 Map p120, B1

In club years, Q Bar is fast approaching retirement age, but big-name guest DJs and a recent renovation

have ensured that it still maintains a place in Bangkok's club scene. (www.qbarbangkok.com; 34 Soi 11, Th Sukhumvit; admission from 300B; ⊙9pm-2am; S Nana exit 3)

Entertainment

Titanium

LIVE MUSIC

29 Map p120, C3

Many come to this cheesy 'ice bar' for the chill, the skimpily dressed working girls and the flavoured vodkas. But we come for Unicorn, the all-female house band, who rock the house every night from 9.30pm to 12.30am. (www.titaniumbangkok.com; 2/30 Soi 22, Th Sukhumvit; ⊙8pm-1am; S Phrom Phong exit 6)

Living Room

LIVE MUSIC

30 Map p120, B2

Don't let looks deceive you: every night from 9.30pm this bland hotel lounge transforms into one of the city's best venues for live jazz. And true to the name, there's comfy, sofa-based seating, all of it within earshot of the music. Enquire ahead of time to see which sax master or hide-hitter is in town. (☑ 0 2649 8888; www.thelivingroomat-bangkok.com; Level 1, Sheraton Grande Sukhumvit, 250 Th Sukhumvit; ⊙6.15pm-midnight; M Sukhumvit exit 3, S Asok exit 2)

Apoteka
LIVE MUSIC

31 Map p120, B1

Antiques and a shoplike setting give Apoteka an old-school feel. Solid drinks and blues bands every night from 9.30pm. (www.apotekabangkok.com; Soi 11, Th Sukhumvit; ⊙5pm-1am Mon-Thu, 5pm-2am Fri-Sat, 3pm-1am Sun; **S**Nana exit 3)

Fat Gut'z
LIVE MUSIC

32 Map p120, G3

This small 'saloon' combines live music and, er, fish and chips. Despite (or perhaps thanks to?) the whiff of chip oil, the odd combo works. Live blues every night from 9pm to midnight. (www.facebook.com/fatgutzsaloon; 264 Soi Thong Lor 12; ⊙5pm-2am; **S**Thong Lo exit 3 & taxi)

Soi Cowboy
RED-LIGHT DISTRICT

33 Map p120, C2

This lane that is filled with raunchy bars claims direct lineage to the post–

Soi Cowboy

Vietnam War R&R era. A real flesh trade functions amid the flashing neon. (Soi Cowboy; ⊙4pm-2am; **M**Sukhumvit exit 2, **S**Asok exit 3)

Nana Entertainment Plaza
RED-LIGHT DISTRICT

34 Map p120, A1

Nana is a go-go bar complex three storeys high, where the sexpats are separated from the gawking tourists. It is also home to a few gà·teu·i (also spelt kàthoey; ladyboys) bars. (Soi 4/Nana Tai, Th Sukhumvit; ⊙4pm-2am; **S**Nana exit 2)

Local Life
Fair-Trade Fair

ThaiCraft Fair (Map p120, C2; www.thaicraft.org; 3rd fl, Jasmine City Bldg, cnr Soi 23 & Th Sukhumvit; ⊙10am-3pm; **M**Sukhumvit exit 2, **S**Asok exit 3) is a great chance to browse through the handicrafts of more than 60 community groups from across Thailand. The fair happens twice a month on Saturdays; check the website to see if the next one is being held during your visit.

Shopping

Shop @ TCDC

HANDICRAFTS

35 Map p120, D3

This shop, attached to the design library/museum of the same name, is a great place to pick up a one of a kind souvenir. A recent visit saw fragrant soaps and candles, kitchen aprons that resemble Thai boxing shorts, unique post cards and cheeky housewares – all dreamt up by Thai designers.

(www.tcdc.or.th/shop; 6th fl, Emporium, cnr Soi 24 & Th Sukhumvit; ⊙10.30am-9pm Tue-Sun; S Phrom Phong exit 2)

Local Life

Bangkok's Savile Row

The strip of Th Sukhumvit between the BTS stops of Nana and Asok is home to some of Bangkok's most famous tailors.

Raja's Fashions (Map p120, B2; ☎0 2253 8379; www.rajasfashions.com; 160/1 Th Sukhumvit; ⊙6.30am-10.30pm Mon-Sat; S Nana exit 4) With his photographic memory for names, Bobby will make you feel as important as the long list of VIPs he has fitted over the decades that he has worked in the tailoring business.

Rajawongse (Map p120, A1; www.dress-for-success.com; 130 Th Sukhumvit; ⊙10.30am-8pm Mon-Sat; S Nana exit 2) Jesse and Victor's creations are particularly renowned among American visitors and residents.

Ricky's Fashion House (Map p120, A1; ☎0 2254 6887; www.rickysfashionhouse.com; 73/5 Th Sukhumvit; ⊙11am-10pm Mon-Sat & 1-5.30pm Sun; S Nana exit 1) Ricky gets positive reviews for his more casual styles of custom-made trousers and shirts.

ZudRangMa Records

MUSIC

Located at Studio Lam (see **22** Map p120, F4), the headquarters of this retro/world label offers a chance to finally combine the university-era pastimes of record-browsing and drinking. Come to snicker at corny old Thai vinyl covers or invest in some of the label's highly regarded compilations of classic *mŏr lam* and *lôok tûng* (Thai-style country music).

(www.zudrangmarecords.com; 7/1 Soi 51, Th Sukhumvit; ⊙2-9pm Tue-Sun; S Thong Lo exit 1)

Nandakwang

HANDICRAFTS

36 Map p120, C2

The Bangkok satellite of a Chiang Mai store, Nandakwang sells a colourful mix of cheery, chunky, hand-embroidered pillows, dolls, bags and other cloth products.

(www.nandakwang.com; 108/2-3 Soi 23, Th Sukhumvit; ⊙9am-6.30pm Mon-Sat; M Sukhumvit exit 2, S Asok exit 3)

Thanon Sukhumvit Market

SOUVENIRS

37 Map p120, B2

Leaving on the first flight out tomorrow morning? Never fear about gifts for those back home; here the street vendors will find you, with handbags, soccer kits, black-felt 'art', sunglasses and jewellery, to name a few. There are also ample stacks of nudie DVDs, Chinese throwing stars, penis-shaped lighters and other questionable gifts for your teenage brother.

(btwn Soi 3 & Soi 15, Th Sukhumvit; ☉11am-11pm Tue-Sun; ⑤Nana exits 1 & 3)

Terminal 21

SHOPPING CENTRE

38 Map p120, C2

Seemingly catering to a Thai need for wacky objects to be photographed in front of, this new mall is worth a visit for the spectacle as much as the shopping. Start at the basement-level 'airport' and proceed upwards through 'Paris', 'Tokyo' and other city-themed floors. Cheesiness aside, it's great for cheap couture, and 'San Francisco' is home to an immense and cheap food court.

(www.terminal21.co.th; cnr Th Sukhumvit & Soi 21/Asoke; ☉10am-10pm; Ⓜ Sukhumvit exit 3, ⑤Asok exit 3)

Almeta

HANDICRAFTS

39 Map p120, C2

If the jewel colours of Thai silk evoke frumpy society matrons, then you're a candidate for Almeta's more muted

Top Tip

Shopping Guide

Bangkok's urban tangle sometimes makes orientation a challenge, and it can be difficult to find out-of-the-way shops and markets. Like having your own personal guide, **Nancy Chandler's Map of Bangkok** (www.nancychandler.net) tracks small, out-of-the-way shopping venues and markets. It also dissects the innards of the Chatuchak Weekend Market (p136). The colourful map is sold in bookshops throughout the city.

earth tones, similar in hue to raw sugar or lotus blossoms.

(www.almeta.com; 20/3 Soi 23, Th Sukhumvit; ☉10am-6pm; Ⓜ Sukhumvit exit 2, ⑤Asoke exit 3)

Sop Moei Arts

HANDICRAFTS

40 Map p120, F2

The Bangkok showroom of this nonprofit organisation features the vibrant cloth creations and baskets of Karen weavers from Mae Hong Son in northern Thailand. Located in the Racquet Club complex Soi 49/9.

(www.sopmoeiarts.com; Soi 49/9, Th Sukhumvit; ☉9.30am-5pm Tue-Sat; ⑤Phrom Phong exit 3 & taxi)

Top Sights
Chatuchak Weekend Market

Getting There

Chatuchak is 6km north of Siam Square.

S BTS Mo Chit exits 1 and 3.

M MRT Chatuchak Park exit 1, and Kamphaeng Phet exits 1 and 2.

Imagine all of Bangkok's markets fused together in a seemingly never-ending commerce-themed barrio. Add a little artistic flair, a saunalike climate and bargaining crowds and you've got a rough sketch of Chatuchak (also spelt 'Jatujak', nicknamed 'JJ'), allegedly one of the world's largest markets. Everything is sold here, from live snakes to *mŏr lam* (Thai folk music) CDs, but the deeper you go, the clearer it becomes that Chatuchak is less about shopping and more about a unique Bangkok experience.

Don't Miss

Accessories

Stalls selling Thai silk, rustic cotton from northern Thailand and hill-tribe bags can be found in Sections 24 and 26. Likewise with stalls selling chunky silver jewellery and semiprecious uncut stones, such as **Orange Karen Silver** (Section 26, Stall 229; ⏰9am-6pm Sat & Sun).

Antiques

Section 1 is the place to go for dusty Buddha statues, old LPs, used books and other random antiques; a string of shops in Section 10, including **Tuptim Shop** (Section 10, Stall 261, Soi 19; ⏰9am-6pm Sat & Sun), sell antique (and new) Burmese lacquerware.

Art

Section 7 is a virtual open-air contemporary art gallery. Works span the spectrum of media, and stalls are frequently changing hands, but we've long liked the Bangkok-themed murals at **Pariwat A-nantachina** (Section 7, Stall 117; ⏰9am-6pm Sat & Sun).

Clothing

Clothing dominates much of Chatuchak, starting in Section 8 and continuing south through the even-numbered sections to Section 24. Sections 5 and 6 deal in used clothing for every Thai youth subculture, from punks to cowboys; Sections 12 and 14 are heavy on hip-hop and skate fashions; Section 4 has heaps of original T-shirts; and Sections 2 and 3 are home to heaps of trendy independent labels.

Eating

Lots of Thai-style eating and snacking will stave off Chatuchak rage (cranky behaviour brought on by dehydration or hunger), and numerous

www.chatuchak.org

Th Phahonyothin

⏰10am-6pm Sat & Sun

☑ Top Tips

▶ Arrive at Chatuchak as early as possible (opening time is approximately 10am), when the crowds are thinner and the temperatures are slightly lower.

▶ An information centre and banks with ATMs and foreign-exchange booths are located just north of Section 1.

✗ Take a Break

There are lots of places to eat in the market; two of our faves are **Foontalop** (Section 26, Stall 319, no roman-script sign; mains 40-100B; ⏰10am-6pm Sat & Sun), a northeastern Thai-style restaurant, and **Café Ice** (Section 7, Stall 267; mains 220-380B; ⏰10am-6pm Sat & Sun), a good place for pàt tai (fried noodles).

food stalls, generally selling snacks and drinks, set up shop just north of Section 19. The majority of sit-down-style restaurants can be found at the periphery of just about every section.

Handicrafts & Souvenirs

A couple of souvenir stalls, such as **Golden Shop** (Section 17, Stall 36; ⊙9am-6pm Sat & Sun), can be found along the western edge of the market, between Sections 17 and 19. For something quirkier, consider a Thai musical instrument at **Kitcharoen Dountri** (Section 8, Stall 464; ⊙9am-6pm Sat & Sun), or miniature models of Thai fruit at **Papachu** (Section 17, Stall 23; ⊙9am-6pm Sat & Sun).

Housewares & Decor

The western edge of the market, particularly along Sections 8 to 26, specialises in all manner of house-

wares, from cheap plastic buckets to expensive brass woks. Stalls in this area, such as **Preecha Ceramic** (Section 19, Stall 196; ⊙10am-6pm), are a particularly good place to stock up on inexpensive Thai ceramics, ranging from celadon-glazed to the traditional rooster-themed bowls from northern Thailand.

Pets

Possibly the most fun you'll ever have window-shopping will be petting puppies and cuddling kittens in Sections 13 and 15. Soi 9 of the former features several shops that deal solely in clothing for pets.

Plants & Gardening

The interior perimeter of Sections 2 to 4 features a huge variety of potted plants, flowers, herbs and fruits, and

Understand
Bargaining

Many of your purchases at Chatuchak Weekend Market will involve an ancient skill that has long been abandoned in the West: bargaining. Contrary to what you may have seen elsewhere, bargaining is not a terse exchange of numbers and animosity. Rather, bargaining Thai style is a generally friendly transaction where two people try to agree on a price that is fair to both of them.

The first rule of bargaining is to have a general idea of the price. Ask around at a few vendors to get a rough notion. When you're ready to buy, it's generally a good strategy to start at 50% of the asking price. If you're buying several of an item, you have much more leverage to request a lower price. If the seller immediately agrees to your first price, you're probably paying too much, but it's bad form to bargain further at this point. Keeping a friendly, flexible demeanour throughout the transaction will almost always work in your favour.

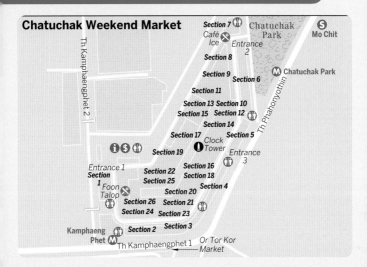

Chatuchak Weekend Market

Th Kamphaengphet 2

Section 7
Café Ice
Entrance 2

Section 8

Section 9
Section 6

Section 11

Section 13 Section 10
Section 15 Section 12

Section 14

Section 17 Section 5

Section 19
Clock Tower
Entrance 3

Entrance 1
Section 1
Section 22 Section 16
Section 25 Section 18

Foon Talop

Section 26 Section 20
Section 24 Section 21
Section 23

Section 2 Section 3

Kamphaeng Phet

Th Kamphaengphet 1

Chatuchak Park
Mo Chit
M Chatuchak Park
Th Phahonyothin

Or Tor Kor Market

the accessories needed to maintain them. Some of these shops are also open on weekday afternoons.

Drinking

Viva 8 (www.facebook.com/Viva8JJ; Section 8, Stall 371; mains 150-300B; ☺9am-10pm Sat & Sun) features a bar, a DJ and a chef making huge platters of paella. Alternatively, as evening draws near, down a beer at **Viva's** (Section 26, Stall 161; ☺10am-10pm Sat & Sun), a cafe-bar that features live music and stays open late.

Nearby: Or Tor Kor Market

Or Tor Kor (องค์กรตลาดเพื่อเกษตรกร; Th Kamphaengphet; ☺8am-6pm; M Kamphaeng Phet exit 3) is Bangkok's highest-quality

fresh market, and taking in sights such as toddler-sized mangoes and dozens of pots full of curries amounts to culinary trainspotting. Head to the market at lunchtime for its open-air food court, which features dishes from across Thailand. It's directly across Th Kamphaengphet from Chatuchak Weekend Market.

Nearby: Chatuchak Park

Chatuchak Park (Th Phahonyothin; admission free; ☺4.30am-9pm; M Chatuchak Park exit 1, Kamphaeng Phet exits 1 & 2, S Mo Chit exit 1 & 3), the weekend market's namesake, is the adjacent, tidy green space – actually a merger of three separate parks – with museums, an artificial lake and bicycles to hire.

Top Sights
Ayuthaya

Getting There

Ayuthaya is about 70km north of Bangkok.

🚐 **Minivan** Depart from a stall east of Bangkok's Victory Monument (60B, one hour, hourly from 5.30am to 9pm).

Ancient ruins, a rural Thai vibe, tasty food, good-value accommodation – and all of this only an hour from Bangkok. Ayuthaya is the easiest and most worthwhile escape from the Big Mango.

Ayuthaya was the capital of Siam from 1350. It was also a major trading port; international merchants visited and were left in awe by the temples and treasure-laden palaces. The glory lasted until 1767, when an invading Burmese army sacked the city, looting most of its treasures. In 1991 Ayuthaya's ruins were designated a Unesco World Heritage Site.

Don't Miss

Ayutthaya Tourist Center

The **Ayutthaya Tourist Center** (📞0 3524 6076; www.
tourismthailand.org/ayutthaya; admission free; ⏰8.30am-
4.30pm) should be your first stop in Ayuthaya, as
the excellent upstairs exhibition hall puts everything in context and describes the city's erstwhile
glories. Also upstairs is the tiny but interesting
Ayutthaya National Art Museum. Downstairs, the
TAT office has lots of maps and good advice.

Ayuthaya Historical Park

The ruins of the former capital, **Ayutthaya
Historical Park**, are one of Thailand's biggest
tourist sites. They're separated into two distinct
districts: the ruins 'on the island' in the central
part of town are most easily visited by bicycle
or motorbike; those 'off the island', opposite the
river from the centre, are best visited by way of
an evening boat tour.

Chao Sam Phraya National Museum

The largest **museum** (พิพิธภัณฑสถานแห่งชาติเจ้า
สามพระยา; cnr Th Rotchana & Th Si Sanphet; adult/child
150B/free; ⏰9am-4pm Wed-Sun; **P**) in the city has
2400 items on show, ranging from a 2m-high
bronze-cast Buddha head to glistening treasures
found in the crypts of Wat Phra Mahathat and
Wat Ratburana.

Ayuthaya Historical Study Centre

This well-designed, open-plan **museum** (ศูนย์ศึกษา
ประวัติศาสตร์อยุธยา; Th Rotchana; adult/child 100/50B;
⏰9am-4.30pm ; **P**) features a diorama of the city's
former glories, replica vessels and an exhibition
on how traditional villagers used to live.

อุทยานประวัติศาสตร์อยุธยา

individual sites 50B,
day passes 220B

⏰8am-5pm

☑ Top Tips

▶ Although buses and
trains also link Bangkok
and Ayuthaya, minivans
are the quickest and
most efficient method of
reaching the city.

✗ Take a Break

Try Ayuthaya's signa-
ture dish, *gǒo·ay đěe·o
reu·a*, aka 'boat noodles',
so-called because they
were formerly sold from
boats, at **Lung Lek** (Th
Chee Kun; mains 30-40B;
⏰8.30am-4pm), located
conveniently across
from Wat Ratburana in
the historical park.

Top Sights
Ko Kret

Getting There

Ko Kret is 15km north of central Bangkok.

🚌 **Bus** Take bus 166 from the Victory Monument to Pak Kret and the cross-river ferry (2B, 5am to 9pm) from the pier at Wat Sanam Neua.

Bangkok's easiest green getaway, Ko Kret is an artificial 'island', the result of a canal being dug nearly 300 years ago to shorten an oxbow bend in Mae Nam Chao Phraya. The island is one of Thailand's oldest settlements of Mon people, who were a dominant tribe of central Thailand between the 6th and 10th centuries AD. Today, Ko Kret is known for its rural atmosphere, distinctive pottery and busy weekend market.

Potter at work, Ko Kret

Don't Miss

Wat Poramai Yikawat

Across from Ko Kret's main pier, **Wat Poramai Yikawat** (Ko Kret; admission free; ⏲9am-5pm), has a Mon-style marble Buddha and a **museum** (Wat Poramai Yikawat, Ko Kret; admission free; ⏲1-4pm Mon-Fri, 9am-5pm Sat & Sun) with religious objects and exhibits on local pottery. But the temple's most famous landmark is undoubtedly the 200-year-old leaning stupa that juts out from the island's northeastern corner.

Pottery

Ko Kret is known for its hand-thrown terracotta pots, sold at markets throughout Bangkok; order an iced coffee from just about any vendor on the island and you'll get a small one as a souvenir. From Wat Poramai Yikawat, go in either direction to find both abandoned kilns and working pottery centres on the east and north coasts.

Touring the Island

A 6km paved path circles Ko Kret, and can be easily completed on foot or by bicycle, the latter available for rent from the pier (40B per day). Alternatively, it's possible to charter a boat for up to 10 people for 500B; the typical island tour stops at a batik workshop, a sweets factory and, on weekends, a floating market.

JOHN BORTHWICK / GETTY IMAGES ©

admission free

☑ Top Tips

▸ Ko Kret can be horribly crowded on weekends; arrive on a weekday instead. There are fewer eating and shopping options, but you'll have the place to yourself.

✕ Take a Break

The northern coast of Ko Kret is home to a row of open-air restaurants, many serving *khâw châa*, an unusual but delicious Mon dish of savoury titbits served with chilled fragrant rice. **Pa Ka Lung** (Restaurant Rever Side; mains 30-60B; ⏲8am-4pm Mon-Fri, to 6pm Sat-Sun), an open-air food court with an English-language menu and sign, serves *khâw châa* and other Thai dishes.

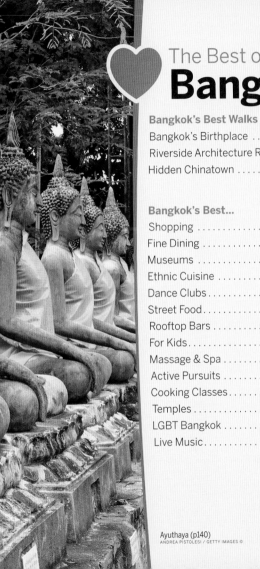

The Best of
Bangkok

Bangkok's Best Walks

Bangkok's Best...

Ayuthaya (p140)
ANDREA PISTOLESI / GETTY IMAGES ©

Best Walks
Bangkok's Birthplace

🏃 The Walk

Most of Bangkok's must-see spots are found in the former royal district, Ko Ratanakosin. This walk takes in all of them, plus some lower-key sights. It's wisest to start early to beat the heat and get in before the hordes descend. Dress modestly in order to gain entry to the temples, and politely but firmly ignore any strangers who approach you offering advice on sightseeing or shopping (p178).

Start 🚤 Tha Chang

Finish 🚤 Wat Arun

Length 4km; three to four hours

🍴 Take a Break

An appropriately old-school lunch break can be had at the long-standing Thai restaurant Ming Lee (p37), located roughly across from the main entrance to Wat Phra Kaew & Grand Palace.

ANDREW WATSON / LONELY PLANET IMAGES ©

Wat Arun (p32)

❶ Silpakorn University

Start at Tha Chang and follow Th Na Phra Lan east with a quick diversion to this institution, Thailand's premier **fine-arts university**.

❷ Wat Phra Kaew & Grand Palace

Continue east to the main gate of **Wat Phra Kaew & Grand Palace** (p24), two of Bangkok's most famous attractions.

❸ Trok Tha Wang

Return to Th Maha Rat and proceed north, through a gauntlet of herbal apothecaries and sidewalk amulet sellers. After passing the cat-laden news-stand (you'll know it when you smell it), turn left into **Trok Tha Wang**, a narrow alleyway holding a seemingly hidden classic Bangkok neighbourhood.

❹ Wat Mahathat

Returning to Th Maha Rat, continue moving north. On your right is **Wat Mahathat**, one of Thailand's most respected Buddhist universities.

❺ Amulet Market

Across the street, turn left into crowded Trok Mahathat to see the cramped **Amulet Market** (p39). As you continue north alongside the river, amulet vendors soon give way to food vendors.

❻ Thammasat University

The emergence of white-and-black uniforms is a clue you're approaching **Thammasat University**, which is known for its law and political-science departments.

❼ Sanam Luang

Exiting at Th Phra Chan, cross Th Maha Rat and continue east until you reach **Sanam Luang**, the 'Royal Field'.

❽ Lak Meuang

Cross the field and continue south along Th Ratchadamnoen Nai until you reach the home of the city spirit of Bangkok, **Lak Meuang**.

❾ Wat Pho

Then head south along Th Sanam Chai and turn right onto Th Thai Wang, which leads to the entrance of **Wat Pho** (p28), home of the giant reclining Buddha.

❿ Wat Arun

If you've still got the energy, head to adjacent Tha Tien to catch the cross-river ferry to **Wat Arun** (p32), one of the few Buddhist temples you're encouraged to climb on.

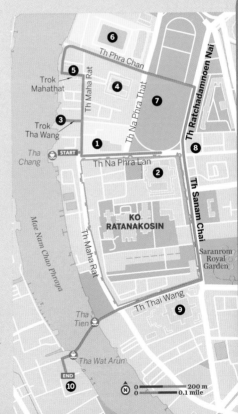

Best Walks
Riverside Architecture Ramble

The Walk

Bangkok isn't generally known for its secular architecture, but the road that parallels Mae Nam Chao Phraya, Th Charoen Krung, is home to many of the city's noteworthy structures. In addition to beautiful buildings, the area was formerly the city's largest foreign enclave, and today continues to serve as a home to many of Bangkok's Muslim residents.

Start [S] Saphan Taksin

Finish Viva & Aviv; [🚢] Tha Si Phraya/River City

Length 3km; two to three hours

Take a Break

Consider lunch or a snack break at Muslim Restaurant (p107), located at the junction of Th Silom and Th Charoen Krung. This eatery dates back at least 70 years and continues to serve tasty halal food.

General Post Office

❶ Shophouses

Starting from the BTS at Saphan Taksin, walk north along Th Charoen Krung, passing the **ancient shophouses** between Th Charoen Wiang and Th Silom.

❷ State Tower

At the corner with Th Silom is the imposing and ugly neoclassical **State Tower**. If it's the afternoon, pop up to the 63rd floor for a drink at **Sky Bar** (p110).

❸ Mandarin Oriental

Turn left on Soi 40, home to the **Mandarin Oriental**, Bangkok's oldest and most storied hotel. The original 1887 structure remains today as the Author's Wing.

❹ East Asiatic Company

Across from the entrance of the Mandarin Oriental is the classical Venetian-style facade of the **East Asiatic Company**, built in 1901.

❺ Assumption Cathedral

Proceed beneath the overhead walkway

linking two buildings to the red-brick **Assumption Cathedral**, which dates back to 1909.

❻ O.P. Place

Return to Soi 40 and take the first left. On your right is **O.P. Place**, today an antique mall, originally built in 1908 to house the German-owned Falck & Beidek Department Store.

❼ Old Customs House

Pass the French Embassy walls and turn left. Head towards the river and the 1890s-era **Old Customs House**.

❽ Haroon Village

Backtrack and turn left beneath the green sign that says 'Haroon Mosque'. You're now in **Haroon Village**, a Muslim enclave.

❾ General Post Office

Wind through Haroon and you'll eventually come to Soi 34, which leads back to Th Charoen Krung. Turn left and cross the street opposite the recently renovated art-deco-style **General Post Office**.

❿ Bangkokian Museum

Head east on Soi 43 until you reach the **Bangkokian Museum** (p102), a compound of three antique wooden homes.

⓫ Viva & Aviv

Cross Th Charoen Krung, enter Soi 30, and continue along Captain Bush Lane to River City – its riverside bar, **Viva & Aviv** (p112), is a good place to end the walk.

Best Walks
Hidden Chinatown

🏃 The Walk

Pencil-thin back lanes, seemingly abandoned shrines, concealed mansions and forgotten neighbourhoods come in spades in this riverside stretch of Bangkok's Chinatown.

Start Holy Rosary Church; 🚤 Tha Si Phraya/ River City

Finish Tha Ratchawong; 🚤 Tha Ratchawong

Length 3km; two to three hours

🍴 Take a Break

If you're doing this walk in the afternoon, consider a drink break at Samsara (p72) located down narrow Soi Khang Wat Pathum Khongkha. If you've got the energy, this walk can be tackled as an extension of the Riverside Architecture Ramble (p148).

Holy Rosary Church

① Holy Rosary Church

Start your walk at the **Holy Rosary Church**, originally located on a plot of land donated to Portuguese Catholics in 1787. Known in Thai as Wat Kalawan, from the Portuguese 'Calvaria', the site of Jesus' crucifixion, the current structure dates to 1898.

② Siam Commercial Bank

Head north along Th Wanit 2; the next compound is the **Siam Commercial Bank**, the country's first domestic bank, dating back to 1910.

③ San Chao Rong Kueak

Head past the Marine Department and turn left on Trok San Chao Rong Kueak; at the end of this lane is the eponymous **Chinese shrine**, a secluded spot for great river views.

④ Jao Sua Son's Mansion

Continue along the riverfront path. Turn left at the first intersection and head north. On your right is the

Chinese-style walled **compound of Jao Sua Son**, a former Chinese 'merchant lord'. Today the mansion is used as a diving school.

⑤ San Jao Sien Khong

Continue north, passing the immense banyan tree. Turn left at the next intersection and follow the path towards the river; this will lead you to **San Jao Sien Khong**, a large Chinese shrine that is mostly quiet save for the annual Vegetarian Festival (p73).

⑥ Talat Noi

Exit the shrine on the north side, turning right on Soi Chow Su Kong, then left on Soi Wanit 2; you're now in the thick of the shophouses and garages of **Talat Noi** (p68).

⑦ Tha Wat Thong Thammachat

Turn right on Th Phanurangsi, then turn left on Th Songwat. Head north briefly, then turn left on Th Song Soem; at the end of this lane is a tiny, unmarked pier. Take the river-crossing ferry (5B,

from 5am to 9pm) to **Tha Wat Thong Thammachat**, just west of where you'll find a semi-enclosed compound of Chinese-style shophouses.

⑧ Th Songwat

Return to the Bangkok side and head west along the crumbling riverside warehouses and shophouses of **Th Songwat**.

⑨ Tha Ratchawong

Turn left on **Th Ratchawong**, where you'll reach the street's eponymous pier, and the end of your walk.

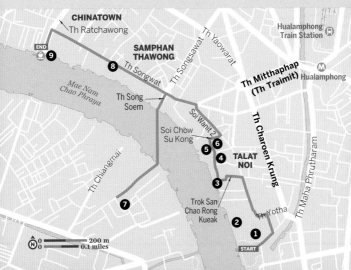

Best
Shopping

Prime your credit card and shine your baht; shopping is serious business in Bangkok. Hardly a street corner in the city is free from a vendor, hawker or impromptu stall, and it doesn't stop there: Bangkok is also home to one of the world's largest outdoor markets, not to mention Southeast Asia's second-largest mall.

Malls & Markets

Although the tourist brochures tend to tout the upmarket malls, Bangkok still lags slightly behind Singapore and Hong Kong in this area. The open-air markets are where the best deals and most original items are found.

Bargaining

At Bangkok's markets and at some of its malls, you'll have to bargain for most, if not all, items. In general, if you see a price tag, it means that the price is fixed and bargaining isn't an option.

Counterfeits

Bangkok is ground zero for the production and sale of counterfeit goods. Keep in mind that counterfeit goods are almost always as shoddy as they are cheap.

Gems & Jewellery

Countless tourists are sucked into a gem scam in which they are taken to a store by a helpful stranger and tricked into buying bulk gems that can supposedly be resold in their home country for 100% profit. The expert con artists seem trustworthy and convince tourists that they need a citizen of the country to circumvent tricky customs regulations. Unsurprisingly, the gem world doesn't work like that, and what most tourists end up with are worthless pieces of glass.

GREG ELMS / GETTY IMAGES ©

☑ Top Tips

▶ **Nancy Chandler's Map of Bangkok** (www.nancychandler. net) is a colourful on-line guide that highlights the quirkier types of shopping venues, which you won't find included on free tourist maps.

Best Markets

Chatuchak Weekend Market One of the world's largest markets and a must-do Bangkok experience. (p137)

Thanon Khao San Market Elephant-print pants, Singha shirts, fresh-squeezed orange juice; all the backpacker essentials are available here. (p57)

Asiatique

Pak Khlong Talat
Bangkok's famous flower
market; come late at
night and don't forget
your camera. (p67)

Talat Mai This frenetic
fresh market is a slice of
China in Bangkok. (p67)

Best for Quirky Souvenirs

Shop @ TCDC
Forward-thinking and
fun Thai souvenirs and
housewares. (p134)

ZudRangMa Records
Pick up some vintage

vinyl or an exotic compil-
ation at the headquarters
of this eponymous record
label. (p134)

Best Malls

MBK Center A seemingly
never-ending Thai market
in a mall. (p91)

Siam Center The place
to go to check in to the
Thai fashion scene. (p91)

Worth a Trip

Bangkok's buzziest
market, **Asiatique**
(www.thaiasiatique.com;
Soi 72-76, Th Charoen
Krung; ⊙4-11pm;
⛴Tha Sathon/Central
Pier) takes the form
of open-air ware-
houses of commerce
next to Mae Nam
Chao Phraya. Expect
clothing, handi-
crafts, souvenirs and
dining and drinking
venues. To get here,
take one of the fre-
quent shuttle boats
from Tha Sathon/
Central Pier.

Best
Fine Dining

Most people associate Bangkok with street food, but the city's eating scene is increasingly diverse, with fine dining establishments ranging in cuisine from French to Thai, including several forays into fusion. And perhaps best of all, this is Bangkok, so happily there's little of the stuffiness associated with fine dining in the West.

MARTIN KREUZER / GETTY IMAGES ©

Best Fine Dining Restaurants

nahm Think upmarket and Thai are mutually exclusive concepts? Watch them come together faultlessly at what is widely considered to be Asia's best restaurant. (p105)

Eat Me Eclectic, eccentric modern cuisine, paired with great service. (p106)

Little Beast Contemporary meals with an endearing American accent. (p122)

Sra Bua A modern, innovative venue where Thai flavours, ingredients and presentation are taken to the next level. (p86)

Four Seasons Sunday Brunch A decadent indulgence and a beloved Bangkok institution. (p87)

Le Du Young Thai culinary upstarts blending local dishes and Western flavours. (p108)

☑ Top Tips

▶ In Bangkok, a reservation is almost never necessary – except for at the venues listed here; be sure to book a table at least a week or two in advance.

▶ Consider visiting Bangkok's fine dining establishments during lunch from Monday to Friday, when two- or three-course set meals can run as little as 400B.

Best
Museums

Bangkok's museums can't compete with those of Europe in terms of collections or sophistication, but the city is home to some unique institutions, ranging from an engaging insight into Siamese culture to a display on forensic science that's quite unlike anything else in the world.

LONELY PLANET / GETTY IMAGES ©

Best Museums

Museum of Siam This fun and interactive museum offers a contemporary look at an ancient culture. (p35)

Yaowarat Chinatown Heritage Center Get the low-down on Thai-Chinese life at this temple-based museum. (p63)

National Museum This expansive compound – a former minor palace – is Thailand's premier repository of national treasures. (p35)

Suan Pakkad Palace Museum This seemingly hidden walled compound is a fascinating depository of ancient Thai art. (p95)

Songkran Niyomsane Forensic Medicine Museum & Parasite Museum As the name matter-of-factly indicates, this is hands down Bangkok's most bizarre museum, and not a destination for the faint of heart. (p36)

Chao Sam Phraya National Museum Treasures from ancient Thailand abound at this upcountry institution. (p141)

Ayuthaya Historical Study Centre Open-plan museum focusing on the daily life of the residents of Siam's former capital. (p141)

☑ **Top Tips**

▶ Student discount cards are generally not recognised in Bangkok; thankfully admission to most institutions remains relatively inexpensive.

▶ Many Bangkok museums are closed on Monday.

Best
Ethnic Cuisine

Contemporary Bangkok's menu extends far beyond Thai; reconsider rice for a meal or two and jump head first into a dining scene where options range from Korean to Egyptian, touching on just about everything in between.

SAM & YVONNE / GETTY IMAGES ©

Asian Cuisines

The bulk of Bangkok's non-Thai restaurants are Asian, predominantly Japanese and, increasingly, Korean. The former can be found across town, but are especially prevalent along Th Sukhumvit, in the areas surrounding BTS Phrom Phong. Korean restaurants can be found on Soi 12, Th Sukhumvit. Bangkok's Chinatown is the place to go for various Chinese cuisines, and South Asian restaurants can be found near the Hindu temple on Th Silom and in Phahurat.

Other Cuisines

The area known as Nana (around Soi 3, Th Sukhumvit) is home to the bulk of Bangkok's Middle Eastern restaurants. French, Italian and other European restaurants are scattered across central Bangkok, but the highest concentration is found along Th Sukhumvit.

☑ **Top Tips**

► Most upmarket restaurants in Bangkok add a 10% service charge to the bill. Some patrons leave extra on top of this charge; others don't – tipping is not obligatory.

► Keep up with the ever-changing international food scene in Bangkok by following the Restaurants section of **BK** (bk.asia-city.com/restaurants) or **Bangkok 101** (www.bangkok101.com).

Best for Ethnic Cuisine

Jidori-Ya Kenzou Chicken skewers grilled over coals with a precision that could only be Japanese. (p122)

Le Beaulieu Fine dining, the French way. (p84)

Shoshana This backpacker staple has been proffering the flavours of Jerusalem for more than 30 years now. (p49)

Din Tai Fung Lauded Taiwanese chain that is *the* place to go for *xiao long bao*, Chinese 'soup' dumplings. (p86)

Chennai Kitchen Bangkok's best southern Indian cuisine. (p107)

Nasir Al-Masri Authentic Egyptian in the heart of Bangkok's Middle Eastern 'hood. (p125)

Best
Dance Clubs

Despite what you may have heard, having a fun night out in Bangkok does not necessarily have to involve ping-pong balls or the word 'go-go'. As in any big international city, the nightlife scene ranges from classy to trashy, and offers just about everything in between.

LONELY PLANET / GETTY IMAGES ©

Bangkok's Club Scene

Bangkok clubs burn strong and bright on certain nights – weekends, or a visit from a foreign DJ or the musical flavour of the month – then hibernate every other night. Hot spots cluster on the soi off Sukhumvit, Silom and RCA (Royal City Avenue), the city's 'entertainment zones', which qualify for the 2am closing time.

Practicalities

Despite the relatively early closing time of 2am, most places don't begin filling up until midnight. Cover charges can run as high as 700B and usually include a drink or two. You'll need ID to prove you're legal (20 years old); they'll card even the grey-haired.

☑ **Top Tips**

▶ To find out what's on when you're in town, go to **BK** (bk.asia-city.com), **Bangkok 101** (www.bangkok101.com), the *Bangkok Post*'s Friday supplement, *Guru*, or **Siam2nite** (www.siam2nite.com).

▶ **Dude Sweet** (www.dudesweet.org), **Club Soma** (www.facebook.com/clubsomaparty) and **Paradise Bangkok** (www.zudrangmarecords.com) are all organisers of hugely popular monthly parties; check their sites to see if anything's on during your stay.

Best Dance Clubs

Grease At press time, this multilevel club wore the crown as Bangkok's best nightclub. (p130)

Arena 10 Where Bangkok's young and beautiful shake their young and beautifuls. (p131)

The Club Dance with a virtual UN of partiers at this Th Khao San–based disco. (p53)

Route 66 This long-standing megaclub on the RCA nightlife strip still manages to draw thousands. (p117)

Glow A boutique disco for discerning dancers. (p131)

Slim A recent face-lift has made this complex the sexy new kid on the block. (p117)

Best
Street Food

Nowhere is the Thai reverence for food more evident than in Bangkok. To the outsider, the life of a Bangkokian appears to be a string of meals and snacks punctuated by the odd stab at work, not the other way around. If you can adjust your guttural clock to this schedule, your stay will be a delicious one indeed.

Street Stalls & Markets

Open-air markets and food stalls are among the most popular dining spots for Thais. In the mornings, stalls selling coffee and Chinese-style doughnuts spring up along busy commuter corridors. At lunchtime, diners might grab a plastic chair at yet another stall for a simple stir-fry. In Bangkok's suburbs, night markets often set up in the middle of town with a cluster of food vendors, metal tables and chairs.

Informal Restaurants

Lunchtime is the right time to point and eat at the typically open-air *ráhn kôw gaang* (rice and curry shops), which sell a selection of premade dishes. The more generic *ráhn ah·hǎhn dahm sàng* (made-to-order restaurant) can often be recognised by a display of raw ingredients and offers a standard repertoire of Thai and Chinese-Thai dishes.

Shophouse Restaurants

Arguably the most delicious type of eatery in Bangkok is the open-fronted shophouse restaurant. The cooks at these places have most likely been serving the same dish for several decades, and really know what they're doing. The food may cost more than that sold from stalls, but the setting is usually more comfortable and hygienic.

TRAVEL INK / GETTY IMAGES ©

☑ Top Tips

▶ Bangkok has passed a citywide ordinance banning street vendors from setting up shop on Mondays, so don't plan on having a street meal on this day of the week.

Best Street Food

Jay Fai Some of the most legendary – and expensive – noodles in town. (p49)

Khun Yah Cuisine The flavours of Bangkok and central Thailand in one convenient location. (p72)

Thip Samai Bangkok's most legendary destination for *pàt tai*. (p50)

Nay Hong Fried noodles unlike anywhere else – if

Chinatown street food

you can find the place. (p72)

Nai Mong Hoi Thod Long-standing hole-in-the-wall serving delicious fried oysters and mussels. (p64)

Lung Lek *The* place to go for Ayuthaya's signature dish. (p141)

Th Phadungdao Seafood Stalls These stalls are so 'street' you risk getting bumped by a car. (p65)

Foontalop Open-air dining in the middle of Chatuchak Weekend Market. (p137)

Pa Aew Ramshackle curry stall in old Bangkok. (p37)

Jék Pûi Curry stall famous for its lack of tables. (p65)

Mangkorn Khŏw Chinatown stall serving excellent wheat and egg noodles. (p65)

Worth a Trip

Are you a vegetarian wanting to experience the flavours of Thai street food? Consider **Baan Suan Pai** (Banana Family Park, Th Phahonyothin; mains 15-30B; ⏰7am-3pm; 🖋; 🆂 Ari exit 1), an open-air food centre with a huge selection of meat-free Thai dishes. To find it, take the BTS to Ari, and after descending at exit 1, turn right down the narrow alleyway just after the petrol station.

Best
Rooftop Bars

Bangkok is one of the few big cities in the world where nobody seems to mind if you slap the odd bar or restaurant on the top of a skyscraper. The options range from chic to cheap and, likewise, range in view from hyperurban to suburban.

PETER ADAMS / GETTY IMAGES ©

Best Rooftop Bars

Moon Bar The combination of casual ambience and stunning views make this our personal fave of Bangkok's original rooftop bars. (p109)

River Vibe Budget guesthouse prices, million-dollar views. (p73)

Roof Sophisticated glances of Mae Nam Chao Phraya and Wat Arun. (p38)

Sky Bar The sweeping Hollywood entrance and seemingly floating bar set the tone at this rooftop venue. (p110)

Sky Train Jazz Club Funky, hidden rooftop bar in a suburban 'hood. (p95)

Phra Nakorn Bar & Gallery Combines views over old Bangkok with some great bar snacks. (p53)

Amorosa Elevated bar with one of Bangkok's best river views. (p39)

☑ Top Tips

▶ Many of Bangkok's rooftop bars won't allow access to those wearing shorts or sandals; dress accordingly.

▶ Forget about lighting up: smoking has been outlawed at all indoor and most outdoor bars and restaurants since 2008.

▶ **Bangkok.com** offers an ever-changing run-down of the city's best rooftop bars (www.bangkok.com/top10-rooftop-bars.htm).

Best
For Kids

STEVE ALLEN /GETTY IMAGES ©

There aren't a whole lot of attractions in Bangkok meant to appeal directly to the little ones, but there's no lack of locals willing to provide attention. This means kids are welcome almost anywhere and you'll rarely experience the sort of eye-rolling annoyance that can occur in the West.

Infants

Nappies (diapers), international brands of milk formula and other infant requirements are widely available. In general, Thai women don't breastfeed in public, though in department stores they'll often find a change room. For moving by foot, slings are often more useful than prams, as Bangkok footpaths are infamously uneven.

Eating with Kids

Dining with children in Thailand, particularly with infants, is a liberating experience, as Thai people are so fond of kids. Take it for granted that your kids will be fawned over, played with, and more often than not, carried around by restaurant waitstaff. It's worth noting that high chairs are rarely found, except at expensive restaurants.

☑ Top Tips

▸ **Bambi** (www.bambi-web.org) is a useful resource for parents and kids in Bangkok.

▸ **Bangkok.com** (www.bangkok.com/kids) includes pages that have a dizzying array of things for kids to do.

Best for Kids

KidZania Vast and modern 'edutainment' complex. (p83)

Lumphini Park Come here for kite flying (in season – February to April), boating and fish feeding. (p102)

Queen Saovabha Memorial Institute Antivenom-producing snake farm. (p102)

Siam Ocean World A huge, kid-friendly aquarium. (p84)

Museum of Siam Lots of interactive exhibits that will appeal to kids. (p35)

Bo.lan This upscale Thai restaurant offers a menu specifically for 'young connoisseurs'. (p123)

Best
Massage & Spa

THOMAS STANKIEWICZ / GETTY IMAGES ©

Bangkok could mount a strong claim to being the massage capital of the world. According to the teachings of traditional Thai healing, the use of herbs and massage should be part of a regular health-and-beauty regimen, not just an excuse for pampering – music to the ears of many a visitor to Bangkok.

Massage or Spa?

In Bangkok, options run from storefront traditional Thai massage to an indulgent spa 'experience' with service and style. And even within the enormous spa category there are choices: there is still plenty of pampering going on, but some spas now focus more on the medical than the sensory, while plush resort-style spas offer a laundry list of specific treatments.

Thai Massage

Although traditional Thai massage (*nôo·at păan boh·rahn*) sounds relaxing, at times it can seem more closely related to Thai boxing than to shiatsu. Thai massage is based on yogic techniques for general health, and involves pulling, stretching, bending, and manipulation of pressure points. Full-body massages usually include camphor-scented balms or herbal compresses, or oil in cheaper establishments. A foot massage is arguably the best way to treat the leg-weariness that comes with sightseeing.

Costs

Depending on the neighbourhood, prices for massages in small parlours run approximately 200B to 350B for an hour-long foot massage, and 300B to 500B for an hour of full-body massage. Spa experiences start at about 800B and climb like a Bangkok skyscraper.

☑ Top Tips

▶ Be forewarned that 'oil massage' is sometimes taken as code for 'sexy massage'.

▶ For summaries of spas not mentioned here, head to the Spa Review page at **Bangkok.com** (www.bangkok.com/spa-reviews).

Best Thai Massage

Health Land Astounding good-value, traditional Thai massage in a clean, contemporary setting. (p103)

Asia Herb Association Massage with an emphasis on Thai-style herbal compresses. (p129)

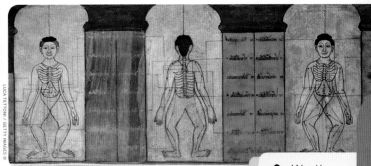

LUCA TETTONI / GETTY IMAGES ©

Historic murals depicting massage pressure points, Wat Pho (p28)

Ruen-Nuad Massage Studio Charming house-bound massage studio. (p102)

Chetawan Traditional Massage School A massage studio in a temple; also home to courses on traditional Thai massage. (p36)

Best Spas

Oriental Spa One of Bangkok's – and Asia's – most lauded spas, although it doesn't come cheap. (p104)

Spa 1930 Cosy spa located in an antique house. (p82)

Thann Sanctuary Chic mall-bound spa employing the eponymous brand's fragrant herbal products. (p84)

Banyan Tree Spa A variety of high-tech spa treatments are available at this hotel spa. (p104)

Worth a Trip

If you've already completed the general course on Thai massage at the **Chetawan Traditional Massage School** (p36), consider the program's more intensive courses, such as Advanced Medical Thai Massage, some of which are held in facilities in Nonthaburi and Nakhon Pathom; check the website for details.

Best
Active Pursuits

JOHN BORTHWICK / GETTY IMAGES ©

Seen all the big sights? Eaten enough *pàt tai* for a lifetime? When you're done soaking it all in, consider some of Bangkok's more active pursuits. Several outfits do bike tours of Chinatown and Ko Ratanakosin, but the top pick are journeys to the rural-feeling Phra Pradaeng Peninsula, just across Mae Nam Chao Phraya.

Best Guided & Speciality Tours

Bangkok Food Tours (📞08 9126 3657; www.bangkokfoodtours.com; tours from 1050B) Culinary wanders around old Bangkok.

Tour with Tong (📞08 1835 0240; www.tourwithtong.com; day tours from 1500B) Recommended guides offering private tours in and around Bangkok.

Bangkok Private Tours (www.bangkokprivatetours.com; half-/full-day walking tours 4700/6000B) Guided walking tours of Bangkok's lesser-known corners.

Thai Private Tour Guide (📞08 2799 1099; www.thaitourguide.com; day tours from 2000B) The guides at this outfit get positive feedback.

Best Bicycle, Segway & Boat Tours

ABC Amazing Bangkok Cyclists (📞0 2665 6364; www.realasia.net; 10/5-7 Soi Aree, Soi 26, Th Sukhumvit; tours from 1300B; ⏱daily tours at 8am, 10am, 1pm & 6pm; 🚇Phrom Phong exit 4) Long-running operation with morning, afternoon and all-day bike tours of Bangkok and its suburbs.

Velo Thailand (📞08 9201 7782; www.velothailand.com; 29 Soi 4, Th Samsen; tours from 1100B; ⏱10am-9pm; 🚤Tha Phra Athit/Banglamphu) Day and night bicycle tours to Thonburi and further afield.

Pandan Tour (📞08 7109 8873, 0 2689 1232; www.thaicanaltour.com; tours from 2395B) Small-boat tours of Bangkok's canals.

Co van Kessel Bangkok Tours

(📞0 2639 7351; www.covankessel.com; ground fl, River City, 23 Th Yotha; tours from 950B; ⏱6am-9pm; 🚤Tha Si Phraya/River City) Dutch-run outfit offering a variety of tours in Chinatown, Thonburi and Bangkok's green zones.

Segway Tour Thailand (📞0 2221 4525; www.segwaytourthailand.com; Maharaj Pier Bldg, Tha Maharaj, off Th Maha Rat; half-day tours 3500B; ⏱8.30am-6.30pm Tue-Sun; 🚤Tha Maharaj) Half-day and full-day Segway tours in and around Bangkok, including among the ruins in Ayuthaya.

Best
Cooking Classes

Consuming everything Bangkok has to offer is one thing, but imagine the points you'll rack up if you can make the same dishes for your friends back at home. A visit to a Thai cooking school has become a must-do on many Bangkok itineraries, and for some visitors it is a highlight of their trip.

JULIET COOMBE / GETTY IMAGES ©

What to Expect

A typical half-day course should include a visit to a fresh market and/or an introduction to Thai ingredients and flavours, and a chance to prepare and cook three or four dishes. Nearly all lessons include a set of printed recipes and end with a communal lunch consisting of your handiwork.

Planning Ahead

Most Bangkok cooking schools offer dishes that change on a daily basis; check the websites to see what dishes are being taught during your visit. Arrange courses at least a couple of days in advance.

Best Cooking Classes

Helping Hands (📞09 4053 7009; www.cook-ingwithpoo.com; courses 1200B; ⏰lessons 8.30am-1pm) This course was started by a native of Khlong Toey's slums and is held in her neighbourhood. Courses span three dishes and include a visit to Khlong Toey Market and transport to and from Th Sukhumvit.

Baipai Thai Cooking School (📞0 2561 1404; www.baipai.com; 8/91 Soi 54, Th Ngam Wong Wan;

courses 2200B; ⏰lessons 9.30am-1.30pm & 1.30-5.30pm) Housed in an attractive villa and taught by a small army of staff, Baipai offers two daily lessons of four dishes. Transport is available.

Blue Elephant Thai Cooking School (📞0 2673 9353; www.blue-elephant.com/cooking-school; 233 Th Sathon Tai, South; courses 2800B; ⏰lessons 8.45am-1.30pm & 1.30-5pm Mon-Sat; 🚇Surasak exit 2) Bangkok's most chichi Thai cooking school offers two lessons daily. The

morning class has a market visit, while the afternoon session includes a detailed introduction to Thai ingredients.

Silom Thai Cooking School (📞08 4726 5669; www.bangkokthaicooking.com; 68 Soi 13, Th Silom; courses 1000B; ⏰lessons 9am-1pm, 1.40-5.30pm & 6-9pm; 🚇Chong Nonsi exit 3) The facilities are basic but Silom crams a visit to a local market and instruction of six dishes into four hours, making it the best bang for your baht.

Best
Temples

A Thai temple (wát) is a compound of different buildings serving specific religious functions. Even if you don't consider yourself spiritual, Bangkok's wát provide pleasures that range in scope from artistic inspiration to urban exploration.

GABRIEL PEREZ / GETTY IMAGES ©

Thai Architecture

Considered the highest art form in Thai society, traditional Thai temple architecture follows relatively strict rules of design that dictate proportion, placement, materials and ornamentation. In addition to the native Siamese styles of building, within Bangkok's temples you'll also find examples from historical Khmer, Mon, Lao and northern Thai traditions.

Buddha Images

Every wát in Bangkok has a Buddha image, which for the most part is sculpted according to strict iconographical rules found in Buddhist art texts dating to the 3rd century AD. There are four basic postures and positions: standing, sitting, walking and reclining.

Temple Murals

A variety of scenes from both secular and religious life embellish the inner walls of temples throughout Bangkok. Always instructional in intent, such painted images range from depictions of the *Jatakas* (life stories of the Buddha) to scenes from the Indian Hindu epic *Ramayana*.

Stupa

Another classic component of Thai temple architecture is the presence of one or more stupa (*chedi* in Thai), a mountain-shaped monument that pays tribute to the enduring stability of Buddhism. Many stupas are said to contain 'relics' (pieces of bone) belonging to the historical Buddha.

MIKEL BILBAO / GETTY IMAGES ©

Wat Arun (p32)

Best Temples

Wat Phra Kaew The granddaddy of Bangkok temples and the home of a certain Emerald Buddha. (p24)

Wat Pho If you haven't seen the ginormous reclining Buddha here, you haven't seen Bangkok. (p28)

Wat Suthat Home to one of Thailand's biggest Buddhas and equally impressive floor-to-ceiling temple murals. (p46)

Wat Traimit Residence of the world's largest golden Buddha. (p62)

Wat Arun This predecessor to Bangkok is also one of the few Thai temples you're allowed to climb on. (p32)

Golden Mount & Wat Saket Hilltop temple with great views over old Bangkok. (p46)

Wat Mangkon Kamalawat The epitome of the hectic, smoky, noisy Chinese-style temple. (p68)

Worth a Trip

Don't have the time to see Thailand's most famous temples? Then consider visiting scaled-down versions of them at **Ancient City** (เมืองโบราณ, Muang Boran; www.ancientcity. com; 296/1 Th Sukhumvit, Samut Prakan; adult/child 500/250B; ⏰8am-5pm), allegedly the largest open-air museum in the world.

Ancient City offers a free shuttle bus from Bearing BTS station, departing at 11.30am on Tuesdays, Thursdays and Saturdays.

Best
LGBT Bangkok

Bangkok has a notoriously pink vibe to it. From kinky male underwear shops mushrooming at street corners to lesbian-only get-togethers, one could eat, shop and play here for days without ever leaving the comfort of gay-friendly venues.

LONELY PLANET / GETTY IMAGES ©

Lesbians

Although it would be a stretch to claim that Bangkok has a lesbian scene, lesbians have become much more open and visible in recent years. It's worth noting that, perhaps because Thailand is still a relatively conservative place, lesbians in Bangkok generally adhere to rather strict gender roles. Overtly 'butch' lesbians, called *tom* (from 'tomboy'), typically have short hair, bind their breasts and wear men's clothing. Femme lesbians refer to themselves as *dêe* (from 'lady'). Visiting lesbians who don't fit into one of these categories may be met with confusion.

Transgender People

Bangkok is famous for its open and visible transgender population – known locally as *gà·teu·i* (also spelt *kàthoey*). Some are cross-dressers, while others have had sexual-reassignment surgery – Thailand is one of the leading countries for this procedure. Foreigners seem to be especially fascinated by trans women, as they are often very convincing women, and *gà·teu·i* cabarets aimed at tourists are wildly popular.

☑ Top Tips

▶ **Bangkok Lesbian** (www.bangkoklesbian.com) is the city's premier website for ladies who love ladies.

▶ **BK** (bk.asia-city.com) and **Siam2nite** (www.siam2nite.com) are good sources for LGBT events in Bangkok.

▶ Bangkok's pride festival appears to be on hiatus, but a good alternative is the biannual party put on by **gCircuit** (www.gcircuit.com).

Cabaret performers

LONELY PLANET / GETTY IMAGES ©

Best for LGBT Travellers

DJ Station One of the most legendary gay dance clubs in Asia. (p99)

Telephone Pub Long-standing and perpetually buzzy pub, right in the middle of Bangkok's pinkest zone. (p98)

Maggie Choo's Sunday is gay day at this otherwise hetero boozer. (p110)

G Bangkok Another booming gay dance club. (p99)

Bearbie The epicentre of Bangkok's bear scene. (p99)

Balcony Streetside watering hole for local and visiting gays. (p98)

Playhouse Theater Cabaret Unapologetically campy transgender stage shows. (p91)

Castro The only gay destination on the nightlife strip known as RCA. (p117)

Worth a Trip

The area around the Lamsalee Intersection, particularly Soi 89/2, Th Rakhamhaeng, is the locals' equivalent of lower Th Silom; expect fun, fly-by-night bars, discos and saunas that will most likely have changed owners and names by the time you read this. To get there, take the MRT to Phra Ram 9, take exit 3 and continue by taxi.

Best
Live Music

Music is an essential element of a Thai night out, and just about every pub worth its salted peanuts has a house band. For the most part this means perky Thai pop covers or international standards, but an increasing number of places have begun to deviate from the norm with quirky and/or original bands and performances.

LONELY PLANET / GETTY IMAGES ©

Bangkok's Live-Music Scene

The local matriarchs and patriarchs like dinner with an easy-listening soundtrack – typically a Filipino band and a synthesiser. An indigenous rock style, *pleng pêu·a chee·wít* ('songs for life'), makes appearances at a dying breed of country-and-western bars decorated with buffalo horns and pictures of Native Americans. Several dedicated bars throughout the city feature blues and rock bands, but are quite scant on live indie performances. For more subdued tastes, Bangkok also attracts grade-A jazz musicians to several hotel bars.

☑ **Top Tips**

▶ To find out if any live shows are happening when you're in town, check in with weekly listings rag **BK** (bk.asia-city. com), **Bangkok 101** (www.bangkok101.com), the *Bangkok Post*'s Friday supplement, *Guru* or **Siam2nite** (www.siam2nite.com/en).

▶ For higher-profile shows, including performances by international artists, check the listings at **ThaiTicketMajor. com** (www.thaiticket-major.com/index_eng. php).

Best Live Music

Titanium Nightly performances by Unicorn, an all-girl band that's bound to get you bouncing. (p132)

Brick Bar Live-music den, famous among locals, for whom dancing on the tables is practically mandatory. (p54)

Living Room As the name suggests, live jazz in a comfortable setting. (p132)

Ad Here the 13th Tiny blues bar in the backpacker district. (p56)

Raintree This earthy suburban pub is a bastion of contemporary Thai folk music. (p95)

Saxophone Pub & Restaurant One of Bangkok's more legendary live-music venues. (p95)

Bamboo Bar Live jazz in a venue with history. (p112)

Survival Guide

Survival Guide

Before You Go

When to Go

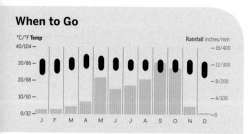

→ Winter (late Dec–early Jan) This is both the coolest time of year in Bangkok and the peak tourist season. Consider November or February for similarly cool weather and fewer people.

→ Wet season (May-Oct) During the monsoon period, Bangkok receives as much as 300mm of rain per month. The good news is that downpours are generally brief and tourist numbers are relatively low.

Book Your Stay

☑ **Top Tip** If your idea of the typical Bangkok hotel was influenced by *The Hangover Part II*, you'll be pleased to learn that the city is home to a diverse spread of modern hostels, guesthouses and hotels. To make matters better, much of Bangkok's accommodation is excellent value, and competition is so intense that fat discounts are almost always available.

Useful Websites

Lonely Planet (www.hotels.lonelyplanet.com) Find reviews and bookings.

Travelfish (www.travelfish.org) Independent reviews with lots of user feedback.

Agoda (www.agoda.com) Advance deals.

Airbnb (www.airbnb.com) Yes, Bangkok is covered here.

Best Budget

➡ **Lub d** (www.lubd.com) A young-feeling, well-run hostel with two branches in central Bangkok.

➡ **NapPark Hostel** (www.nappark.com) High-tech dorm beds in a hostel with a distinct emphasis on activities.

➡ **Sam Sen Sam Place** (www.samsensam) Cutesy budget rooms in an antique wooden home by the river.

➡ **Chern** (www.chernbangkok.com) A modern hostel, including huge private rooms, has been coaxed out of this former factory.

Best Midrange

➡ **Lamphu Treehouse** (www.lamphutreehotel.com) Quiet, comfy, canal-side midranger just outside Bangkok's backpacker zone.

➡ **Phra-Nakorn Norn-Len** (www.phra-korn-nornlen.com) An arty, fun hotel compound in a refreshingly untouristed 'hood.

➡ **Smile Society** (www.smilesocietyhostel.com) This four-storey shophouse in 'new' Bangkok combines small but comfortable rooms

and dorms and helpful, service-minded staff.

➡ **Napa Place** (www.napaplace.com) Modern condo-like hotel with big rooms and a homey vibe.

➡ **Feung Nakorn Balcony** (www.feungnakorn.com) A former school holding 42 bright, cheery rooms.

➡ **Glow Trinity Silom** (www.zinchospitality.com/glowbyzinc/silom) A sophisticated-feeling hotel at a midrange price.

Best Top End

➡ **Peninsula** (www.peninsula.com/bangkok) Frequently one of the highest-ranking luxury hotels in the world.

➡ **AriyasomVilla** (www.ariyasom.com) Sumptuous refurbished villa with a classy B&B vibe.

➡ **Metropolitan by COMO** (www.comohotels.com/metropolitanbangkok) Sophisticated urban cool in the centre of the city.

➡ **Mandarin Oriental** (www.mandarinoriental.com/bangkok) The *grande dame* of Bangkok hotels still delivers after 135 years.

Arriving in Bangkok

☑ **Top Tip** For the best way to get to your accommodation, see p17.

Suvarnabhumi International Airport

➡ Just about everybody flying to Bangkok comes through **Suvarnabhumi International Airport** (BKK; ✆ 0 2132 1888; www.suvarnabhumiairport.com), located 25km east of the city centre.

➡ Pronounced *sù·wan·ná·poom*, Suvarnabhumi airport is accessible by taxi and public transport – including the **Airport Rail Link** (www.bangkokairportrain.com) – and transit time to most parts of Bangkok is approximately 30 to 45 minutes. A taxi to central Bangkok will run about 300B.

➡ The unofficial website has real-time details of airport arrivals and departures. Left-luggage facilities are available on level 2, beside the helpful Tourism Authority of Thailand (TAT) office (p180).

Don Muang International Airport

➜ Bangkok's former hub, **Don Muang International Airport** (DMK; ☎0 2535 1111; www.donmuangairportonline.com), has been downgraded to the city's de facto low-cost airport. It's located about 20km north of the city centre; slow buses make the trip into town, but taxi is the most efficient way to get to/from the airport, and to central Bangkok should cost around 200B.

Hualamphong Train Station

➜ **Hualamphong Station** (☎0 2220 4334, call centre 1690; www.railway.co.th; off Th Phra Ram IV; M Hua Lamphong exit 2) is the city's main train terminal, and is linked to the MRT (metro) stop at Hua Lamphong.

Travel Passes

Both the BTS and MRT offer unlimited-ride one-day passes for 130B.

Bus

➜ Bangkok's main bus terminals are all located at different ends of the city, and all most conveniently linked to the various parts of town by taxi.

➜ **Northern & Northeastern Bus Terminal** (Mo Chit; ☎northeastern routes 0 2936 2852, ext 602/605, northern routes 0 2936 2841, ext 325/614; Th Kamphaeng Phet; M Kamphaeng Phet exit 1 & taxi, S Mo Chit exit 3 & taxi)

➜ **Eastern Bus Terminal** (Ekamai; Map p120, G5; ☎0 2391 2504; Soi 40, Th Sukhumvit; S Ekkamai exit 2)

➜ **Southern Bus Terminal** (Sai Tai Mai; ☎0 2894 6122; Th Boromaratchachonanee)

Getting Around

BTS & MRT
☑ **Best for...** Getting between points in central Bangkok and getting around during peak hours.

➜ The elevated **BTS** (☎0 2617 7300, tourist information 0 2617 7340; www.bts.co.th), also known as the Skytrain, whisks you through 'new' Bangkok (Silom, Sukhumvit and Siam Sq). The interchange is at Siam station, and trains run frequently from 6am to midnight. Fares range from 15B to 52B. Most ticket machines only accept coins, but change is available at the information booths.

➜ Bangkok's metro, the **MRT** (www.bangkokmetro.co.th) helps people who are staying in the Sukhumvit or Silom area reach Chinatown or the train station at Hualamphong. Fares cost 16B to 40B. The trains run frequently from 6am to midnight.

Taxi
☑ **Best for...** Getting from one part of town to another at nonpeak hours.

➜ Although many first-time visitors are hesitant to use them, in general, Bangkok's taxis are new and comfortable and the drivers are courteous and helpful, making them an excellent way to get around.

➡ All taxis are required to use their meters, which start at 35B, and fares to most places within central Bangkok cost 60B to 90B. Freeway tolls – 25B to 60B depending on where you start – must be paid by the passenger.

➡ **Taxi Radio** (☏1681; www.taxiradio.co.th) and other 24-hour 'phone-a-cab' services are available for 20B above the metered fare; and Uber, GrabTaxi and other similar services are gaining popularity.

Boat

☑ **Best for...** Slowly but surely jumping between the tourist sights that are located in Banglamphu, Ko Ratanakosin and parts of Silom.

➡ The **Chao Phraya Express Boat** (☏0 2623 6001; www.chaophrayaexpressboat.com) runs from 6am to 10pm. You can buy tickets (10B to 40B) at the pier or on board; hold on to your ticket as proof of purchase. Boats with yellow or red-and-orange flags are express boats. These run only on weekdays during peak times and don't make every stop. A blue-flagged tourist boat runs

from Asiatique or Tha Sathon/Central Pier to Tha Phra Athit/Banglamphu with stops at major sightseeing piers and barely comprehensible English-language commentary.

➡ There are also dozens of cross-river ferries, which charge 3B and run every few minutes from approximately 6am to 9pm.

➡ *Klorng* (canal, also spelled *khlong*) taxi boats run along Khlong Saen Saeb (Banglamphu to Ramkhamhaeng) and are an easy way to get between Banglamphu and Jim Thompson House, the Siam Sq shopping centres and other points further east along Th Sukhumvit – after a mandatory change of boat at Pratunam Pier. These boats are mostly used by daily commuters and pull into the piers for just a few seconds – jump straight on or you'll be left behind. Fares range from 10B to 20B and boats run from 5.30am to 8.30pm Monday to Friday, and from 6am to 7.15pm on weekends.

Motorcycle Taxi

☑ **Best for...** Getting to the end of a long street or getting somewhere in a hurry during peak hours.

➡ Motorcycle taxis (colloquially known as *motorsai*) serve two purposes in Bangkok. Most commonly and popularly they form an integral part of the public transport network, running from the corner of a main thoroughfare, such as Th Sukhumvit, to the far ends of soi that run off that thoroughfare. Riders wear coloured vests that are numbered and gather at either end of their soi, usually charging 10B to 20B for the trip (without a helmet unless you ask for one).

➡ Their other purpose is as a means of beating the traffic. You tell your rider where you want to go, negotiate a price (from 20B for a short trip up to about 150B for going across town), strap on the helmet (they will insist for longer trips) and say a prayer to whichever god you're into.

Túk-Túk

☑ **Best for...** Short hops within a neighbourhood.

➡ These putt-putting three-wheeled vehicles are irresistible tourist-traps – they'll zip you to an overpriced tailor or jeweller regardless of your stated destination. Refuse to enter any unrequested shop, and skip the 10B sightseeing offers.

Bus

☑ **Best for...** Reaching Banglamphu, Dusit and other areas not serviced by the BTS or MRT.

➡ Bangkok's public buses are run by the **Bangkok Mass Transit Authority** (☎0 2246 0973; www.bmta.co.th). As the routes are not always clear, and with Bangkok taxis being such a good deal, you'd really have to be pinching pennies to rely on buses as a way to get around Bangkok. However, if you're determined, air-con bus fares range from 11B to 30B, and fares for fan-cooled buses start at 7B or 8B. Most of the bus lines run between 5am and 10pm or 11pm.

Essential Information

Business Hours

☑ **Top Tip** Although most Bangkok banks close by 3.30pm, those in shopping centres and tourist areas are often open longer hours (generally until 8pm), including weekends.

Banks From 9.30am to 3.30pm Monday to Friday.

Bars & Clubs Open until midnight or 1am, although those in designated entertainment zones may stay open until 2am.

Restaurants Local Thai places often serve food from morning until night (10am to 8pm or 9pm), while more formal restaurants serve only during lunch (from around 11am to 2pm) and dinner (6pm to 10pm).

Shops Large shops usually open from 10am to 7pm; shopping centres open until 10pm.

Electricity

220V/50Hz

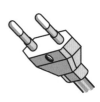

220V/50Hz

Emergency

☑ **Top Tip** Although Thailand has a medical emergency number (☎191), it's probably best to call a hospital direct, and it will dispatch an ambulance.

➡ **Tourist Police** (☎24hr hotline 1155) The best way to deal with most problems requiring police (usually a rip-off or theft) is to contact the tourist police, who can generally communicate in English, are used to dealing with foreigners and can be very helpful in cases of arrest.

Money

☑ **Top Tip** Tipping is not a traditional part of Thai life; except in big hotels and posh restaurants, tips are appreciated but not expected.

Currency

➡ The basic unit of Thai currency is the baht. There are 100 satang in one baht.

➡ Coins come in denominations of 25 satang, 50 satang, 1B, 2B, 5B and 10B.

➡ Paper currency comes in denominations of 20B (green), 50B (blue), 100B (red), 500B (purple) and 1000B (beige).

ATMs

☑ **Top Tip** You won't need a map to find an ATM in Bangkok – they're literally everywhere.

➡ ATMs accept major international credit cards and many will also cough up cash (Thai baht only) if your card is affiliated with the international Cirrus or Plus networks (typically for a fee ranging from 150B to 180B).

➡ You can withdraw a maximum of 20,000B per day from most ATMs.

Credit Cards

➡ Credit cards as well as debit cards can be used for purchases at many shops and pretty much any hotel or restaurant, though you'll have to pay cash for your *pàt tai*.

➡ The most commonly accepted cards are Visa and MasterCard, followed by Amex and JCB.

Money Changers

➡ Banks or legal money changers offer the optimum foreign-exchange rates.

➡ When buying baht, US dollars and euros are the most readily accepted currencies; travellers cheques receive better rates than cash.

➡ British pounds, Australian dollars, Singapore dollars and Hong Kong dollars are also widely accepted.

Public Holidays

Government offices and banks close their doors on the following national public holidays. For the precise dates of lunar holidays, see the Tourism Authority of Thailand (TAT) website, www.tourismthailand.org/See-and-Do/Events-and-Festivals.

1 January New Year's Day

February (date varies) Makha Bucha Day, Buddhist holy day

6 April Chakri Day, commemorates the founding of the royal Chakri dynast

13–15 April Songkran Festival, Thai New Year and water festival

1 May Labor Day

5 May Coronation Day, commemorating the 1946 coronation of the current king and queen

May/June (date varies) Visakha Bucha Day, Buddhist holy day

July (date varies) Asanha Bucha, beginning of the Buddhist 'lent'

12 August Queen's Birthday/Mother's Day

23 October Chulalongkorn Day

October/November (date varies) Ork Phansa, end of Buddhist 'lent'

5 December King's Birthday/Father's Day

10 December Constitution Day

31 December New Year's Eve

Safe Travel

Bangkok is generally a safe city and incidents of violence against tourists are rare. That said, there are enough well-rehearsed scams that there's an entire website (www.bangkokscams.com) dedicated to them. But don't be spooked by the stories; commit the following to memory and you'll most likely enjoy a scam-free visit:

➡ **Gem scam** We are begging you, if you aren't a gem trader or expert, then please don't buy unset stones in Thailand – period. Otherwise, you'll find yourself getting sucked into a complicated scam in which you'll pay an exorbitant price for costume jewellery.

➡ **Closed today** Ignore any 'friendly' local who tells you that an attraction is closed for a Buddhist holiday or for cleaning. These are set-ups for trips to a bogus gem sale.

➡ **Túk-túk rides for 10B** Say goodbye to your day's itinerary if you climb aboard this ubiquitous scam. These alleged 'tours' bypass all the sights and instead cruise to all the fly-by-night gem and tailor shops that pay commissions.

➡ **Flat-fare taxi ride** Flatly refuse any taxi driver who quotes a flat fare (usually between 100B and 150B for in-town destinations), which will usually be three times more expensive than the reasonable meter rate. Walking beyond the tourist area will usually help you find an honest driver.

➡ **Friendly strangers** Be wary of smartly dressed and well-spoken men who approach you asking where you're from and where you're going. Their opening gambit is usually followed with: 'Ah, my son/daughter is studying at university in (your home city)' – they seem to have an encyclopaedic knowledge of the world's major universities. As the tourist authorities here have pointed out, this sort of behaviour is out of character for Thais and should be treated with suspicion.

Telephone

Mobile Phones

➡ If you have a GSM phone you will probably be able to use it on roaming in Thailand. If you have endless cash, or you only want to send text messages, you might be happy to do that. Otherwise, think about buying a local SIM card.

➡ If your phone is locked, head down to MBK Center (p91) to get it unlocked or to shop for a new or cheap used phone (they start at less than 2000B).

➡ Buying a prepaid SIM is as easy as finding a 7-Eleven. The market is supercompetitive and deals vary so check websites first, but expect to get a SIM for as little as 49B. More expensive SIMs might come with preloaded talk time; if not, recharge cards are sold at the same stores and start at 10B.

Making International & Domestic Calls

➔ Inside Thailand you must dial the area code no matter where you are. In effect, that means all numbers are nine digits; in Bangkok they begin with ☎02, and are followed by a seven-digit number. The only time you drop the initial ☎0 is when you're calling from outside Thailand.

➔ To direct-dial an international number from a private phone, you can first dial ☎001 then the country code. However, you wouldn't do that, because ☎001 is the most expensive way to call internationally, and numerous other prefixes give you cheaper rates. These include ☎007, ☎008 and ☎009, depending on which phone you're calling from. If you buy a local mobile-phone SIM card, the network provider will tell you which prefix to use; read the fine print.

Useful Numbers

Thailand Country Code
☎66
Bangkok city code ☎02
Mobile numbers ☎06, ☎08, ☎09
Operator-assisted international calls ☎100
Free local directory assistance call ☎1133

Toilets

☑ **Top Tip** Toilet paper is rarely provided, so carry an emergency stash.

➔ If you don't want to pee against a tree like the túk-túk drivers, you can stop in at any shopping centre, hotel or fast-food restaurant for facilities. Shopping centres typically charge 3B for a visit.

➔ In older buildings and wát you'll still find squat toilets, but in modern Bangkok expect to be greeted by a throne.

➔ Even in places where sit-down toilets are installed, the septic system may not be designed to take toilet paper. In such cases there will be a waste basket where you're supposed to place used toilet paper and feminine

Dos & Don'ts

➔ Don't say anything critical about the Thai royal family.

➔ Do dress respectfully at royal buildings and temples.

➔ Don't wear your shoes indoors.

➔ Do try to avoid conflict or raising your voice with locals.

➔ Don't touch another person's head.

hygiene products. Many toilets also come with a small spray hose – Thailand's version of the bidet.

Tourist Information

Bangkok has two organisations that handle tourism matters: the Tourism Authority of Thailand (TAT) for country-wide information and the Bangkok Information Center for city-specific advice.

Bangkok Information Center (Map p34 C1; ☎0 2225 7612-4; www.bangkoktourist.com; 17/1 Th Phra Athit; ⏰9am-7pm

Mon-Fri, to 5pm Sat & Sun; 🚊Tha Phra Athit (Banglamphu)) Provides maps, brochures and directions. Kiosks and booths are found around town; look
for the green-on-white symbol of a mahout on an elephant.

Tourism Authority of Thailand (TAT; 📞1672; www.tourismthailand. org) Has branches in Banglamphu (📞0 2283 1500; cnr Th Ratchadamnoen Nok & Th Chakrapatdipong; ⏰8.30am-4.30pm; 🚊klorng boatPhanfa Leelard Pier) and at Suvarnabhumi International Airport (📞0 2134 0040; 2nd fl, btwn Gates 2 & 5; ⏰24hr).

Travellers with Disabilities

➡ With its high kerbs, uneven pavements and nonstop traffic, Bangkok presents one large, on-going obstacle course for the mobility-impaired. Many of the city's streets must be crossed via pedestrian bridges flanked with steep stairways, while buses and boats don't stop long enough to accommodate even the mildly disabled. Apart from some BTS and MRT stations, ramps or other access points for wheelchairs are rare.

➡ A few top-end hotels make consistent design efforts to provide disabled access. Other deluxe hotels with high employee-to-guest ratios are usually good about providing staff help where building design fails. For the rest, you're pretty much left to your own resources.

➡ The following companies and websites might be useful: **Asia Pacific Development Centre on Disability** (www.apcd-foundation.org), **Society for Accessible Travel & Hospitality** (SATH; www. sath.org) and **Wheelchair Holidays @ Thailand** (www.wheelchairtours.com).

Visas

➡ Thailand's **Ministry of Foreign Affairs** (www.mfa. go.th) oversees immigration and visa issues. In the past five years there have been new rules nearly every year regarding visas and extensions; the best online monitor is **Thaivisa** (www.thaivisa. com).

➡ Citizens of 41 countries (including most European countries, Australia, New Zealand and the USA) can enter Thailand at no charge. These citizens are issued a 30-day visa exemption if they arrive by air, or a 15-day exemption if they arrive by land.

Language

In Thai the meaning of a single syllable may be altered by means of different tones. Standard Thai has five tones: low (eg *bàht*), mid (eg *dee*), falling (eg *mâi*), high (eg *máh*) and rising (eg *săhm*). The range of all five tones is relative to each speaker's vocal range, so there is no fixed 'pitch' intrinsic to the language.

Read our pronunciation guides as if they were English and you'll be understood. The hyphens indicate syllable breaks; some syllables are further divided with a dot to help you pronounce compound vowels (eg *mêu·a·rai*). Note that **b** is a hard 'p' sound, almost like a 'b' (eg in 'hip-bag'); **d** is a hard 't' sound, like a sharp 'd' (eg in 'mid-tone'); **ng** is pronounced as in 'singing', but in Thai it can also occur at the start of a word; and **r** is pronounced as in 'run' but flapped, and in everyday speech it's often pronounced like 'l'.

To enhance your trip with a phrasebook, visit **lonelyplanet.com**. Lonely Planet iPhone phrasebooks are available through the Apple App store.

Basics

Hello.	สวัสดี	sà-wàt-dee
Goodbye.	ลาก่อน	lah gòrn
Yes./No.	ใช่/ไม่	châi/mâi
Please.	ขอ	kŏr
Thank you.	ขอบคุณ	kòrp kun
You're welcome.	ยินดี	yin dee
Excuse me.	ขออภัย	kŏr à-pai
Sorry.	ขอโทษ	kŏr tôht

How are you?
สบายดีไหม	sà-bai dee măi

Fine. And you?
สบายดีครับ/ค่ะ	sà-bai dee kráp/
แล้วคุณล่ะ	kâ láa·ou kun lâ (m/f)

Do you speak English?
คุณพูดภาษา	kun pôot pah-săh
อังกฤษได้ไหม	ang-grìt dâi măi

I don't understand.
ผม/ดิฉันไม่	pŏm/dì-chăn mâi
เข้าใจ	kôw jai (m/f)

Eating & Drinking

I'd like (the menu), please.
ขอ (รายการ	kŏr (rai gahn
อาหาร) หน่อย	ah-hăhn) nòy

I don't eat ...
ผม/ดิฉัน	pŏm/dì-chăn
ไม่กิน ...	mâi gin ... (m/f)

eggs	ไข่	kài
fish	ปลา	blah
red meat	เนื้อแดง	néu·a daang
nuts	ถั่ว	tòo·a

That was delicious!
อร่อยมาก	à-ròy mâhk

Cheers!
ไชโย	chai-yoh

Please bring the bill.
ขอบิลหน่อย	kŏr bin nòy

cafe	ร้านกาแฟ	ráhn gah-faa
market	ตลาด	đà-làht
restaurant	ร้านอาหาร	ráhn ah-hăhn
vegetarian	คนกินเจ	kon gin jair

Meat & Fish

beef	เนื้อ	néu·a
chicken	ไก่	gài
crab	ปู	boo
duck	เป็ด	bèt
fish	ปลา	blah
meat	เนื้อ	néu·a
pork	หมู	mŏo
seafood	อาหารทะเล	ah-hăhn tá-lair
squid	ปลาหมึก	blah mèuk

Fruit & Vegetables

banana	กล้วย	glôo·ay
beans	ถั่ว	tòo·a
coconut	มะพร้าว	má-prów
eggplant	มะเขือ	má-kěu·a
fruit	ผลไม้	pŏn-lá-mái
guava	ฝรั่ง	fa-ràng
lime	มะนาว	má-now
mango	มะม่วง	má-môo·ang
mangosteen	มังคุด	mang-kút
mushrooms	เห็ด	hèt
nuts	ถั่ว	tòo·a
papaya	มะละกอ	má-lá-gor
potatoes	มันฝรั่ง	man fa-ràng

rambutan	เงาะ	ngó
tamarind	มะขาม	má-kăhm
tomatoes	มะเขือเทศ	má-kěu·a têt
vegetables	ผัก	pàk
watermelon	แตงโม	đaang moh

Drinks

beer	เบียร์	bee·a
coffee	กาแฟ	gah-faa
milk	นมจืด	nom jèut
orange juice	น้ำส้ม	nám sôm
soy milk	น้ำเต้าหู้	nám đôw hôo
sugar-cane juice	น้ำอ้อย	nám ôy
tea	ชา	chah
water	น้ำดื่ม	nám dèum

Other

chilli	พริก	prík
egg	ไข่	kài
fish sauce	น้ำปลา	nám blah
noodles	เส้น	sên
pepper	พริกไทย	prík tai
rice	ข้าว	kôw
salad	ผักสด	pàk sòt
salt	เกลือ	gleu·a
soup	น้ำซุป	nám súp
soy sauce	น้ำซีอิ๊ว	nám see-éw
sugar	น้ำตาล	nám đahn
tofu	เต้าหู้	đôw hôo

Shopping

I'd like to buy ...
อยากจะซื้อ ... yàhk jà séu ...

How much is it?
เท่าไร tôw-rai

That's too expensive.
แพงไป paang Ƀai

Can you lower the price?
ลดราคาได้ไหม lót rah-kah dâi măi

There's a mistake in the bill.
บิลใบนี้ผิด bin bai née pìt ná
นะครับ/ค่ะ kráp/kâ (m/f)

Emergencies

Help! ช่วยด้วย chôo·ay dôo·ay

Go away! ไปให้พ้น Ƀai hâi pón

Call a doctor!
เรียกหมอหน่อย rêe·ak mŏr nòy

Call the police!
เรียกตำรวจหน่อย rêe·ak đam·ròo·at nòy

I'm ill.
ผม/ดิฉัน pŏm/dì-chăn
ป่วย Ƀòo·ay (m/f)

I'm lost.
ผม/ดิฉัน pŏm/dì-chăn
หลงทาง lŏng tahng (m/f)

Where are the toilets?
ห้องน้ำอยู่ที่ไหน hôrng nám yòo têe năi

Time, Days & Numbers

What time is it?
กี่โมงแล้ว gèe mohng láa·ou

morning	เช้า	chów
afternoon	บ่าย	bài
evening	เย็น	yen
yesterday	เมื่อวาน	mêu·a wahn
today	วันนี้	wan née
tomorrow	พรุ่งนี้	prûng née
Monday	วันจันทร์	wan jan
Tuesday	วันอังคาร	wan ang-kahn
Wednesday	วันพุธ	wan pút
Thursday	วันพฤหัสฯ	wan pá-réu-hàt
Friday	วันศุกร	wan sùk
Saturday	วันเสาร์	wan sŏw
Sunday	วันอาทิตย์	wan ah-tít
1	หนึ่ง	nèung
2	สอง	sŏrng
3	สาม	săhm
4	สี่	sèe
5	ห้า	hâh
6	หก	hòk
7	เจ็ด	jèt
8	แปด	Ƀàat
9	เก้า	gôw
10	สิบ	sìp
20	ยี่สิบ	yêe-sìp
21	ยี่สิบเอ็ด	yêe-sìp-èt

30	สามสิบ	săhm-sìp
40	สี่สิบ	sèe-sìp
50	ห้าสิบ	hâh-sìp
60	หกสิบ	hòk-sìp
70	เจ็ดสิบ	jèt-sìp
80	แปดสิบ	ɓàat-sìp
90	เก้าสิบ	gôw-sìp
100	หนึ่งร้อย	nèung róy
1000	หนึ่งพัน	nèung pan
1,000,000	หนึ่งล้าน	nèung láhn

Transport & Directions

Where is ...?

... อยู่ที่ไหน ... yòo têe năi

What's the address?

ที่อยู่คืออะไร têe yòo keu à-rai

Can you show me (on the map)?

ให้ดู (ในแผนที่) hâi doo (nai păan têe)
ได้ไหม dâi măi

Turn left/right.

เลี้ยวซ้าย/ขวา lée·o sái/kwăh

bicycle rickshaw	สามล้อ	săhm lór
boat	เรือ	reu·a
bus	รถเมล์	rót mair
car	รถเก๋ง	rót gĕng
motorcycle	มอร์เตอร์ไซค์	mor-đeu-sai
taxi	รับจ้าง	ráp jâhng
plane	เครื่องบิน	krêu·ang bin
train	รถไฟ	rót fai
túk-túk	ตุ๊ก ๆ	đúk đúk

When's the first bus?

รถเมล์คันแรก rót mair kan râak
มาเมื่อไร mah mêu·a rai

A (one-way/return) ticket, please.

ขอตั๋ว (เที่ยว kŏr đŏo·a (têe·o
ดียว/ไปกลับ) dee·o/ɓai glàp)

What time does it get to ...?

ถึง ... กี่โมง tĕung ... gèe mohng

Does it stop at ...?

รถจอดที่ ... ไหม rót jòrt têe ... măi

I'd like to get off at ...

ขอลงที่ ... kŏr long têe ...

Behind the Scenes

Send Us Your Feedback

We love to hear from travellers – your comments help make our books better. We read every word, and we guarantee that your feedback goes straight to the authors. Visit **lonelyplanet.com/contact** to submit your updates and suggestions.

Note: We may edit, reproduce and incorporate your comments in Lonely Planet products such as guidebooks, websites and digital products, so let us know if you don't want your comments reproduced or your name acknowledged. For a copy of our privacy policy visit lonelyplanet.com/privacy.

Austin's Thanks

Big thanks to DE Sarah Reid and super carto Diana Von Holdt, as well as to the kind folks on the ground in Bangkok.

Acknowledgments

Cover photograph: Wat Arun, Bangkok, Jon Arnold/AWL.

This Book

This 5th edition of Lonely Planet's *Pocket Bangkok* guidebook was researched and written by Austin Bush, who also wrote the previous three editions.

This guidebook was produced by the following:

Destination Editor Sarah Reid **Product Editors** Alison Ridgway, Luna Soo **Regional Senior Cartographer** Diana Von Holdt **Book Designer** Cam Ashley **Assisting Editors** Imogen Bannister, Bruce Evans, Gabrielle Stefanos **Cover Researcher** Naomi Parker

Thanks to Louise Bastock, Kate Chapman, Anna Harris, Elizabeth Jones, Claire Naylor, Karyn Noble, Katie O'Connell, Andrea Pappin, Giovanni Serrapere, Ellie Simpson, Lawrie Smith, Lauren Wellicome, Tony Wheeler

Index

See also separate subindexes for:

✖ **Eating p188**

🍸 **Drinking p189**

✿ **Entertainment p190**

🛍 **Shopping p190**

Eating

Our Writer

Austin Bush

Austin Bush came to Thailand in 1999 as part of a language study program hosted by Chiang Mai University. The lure of city life, employment and spicy food eventually led him to Bangkok. City life, employment and spicy food have managed to keep him there since. A native of Oregon, USA, Ausin is a writer and photographer who often focuses on food. Samples of his work can be seen at www.austinbushphotography.com.

Published by Lonely Planet Publications Pty Ltd
ABN 36 005 607 983
5th edition – June 2015
ISBN 978 1 74321 672 9
© Lonely Planet 2015 Photographs © as indicated 2015
10 9 8 7 6 5 4
Printed in Singapore